"HIGH TECH" isn't just the wave of the future, says Bob Slocum—it's here. And Christians who want to have a vital, life-changing ministry in their world must come to terms with that fact. Furthermore, it is up to the laity—ordinary Christians, not church "professionals"—to explore a new positive future for the church in the coming decades.

In this book, Bob Slocum speaks as both a high-tech professional and a committed Christian, challenging his fellow lay men and women to develop inner resources and external strategies that can make a difference in their churches and their world.

A guaranteed discussion starter for study groups (complete with built-in study guide), this book is also wonderful for individual reading. But beware. You may read it on your own, but you probably won't be able to keep it to yourself! Why fight it? Read this book, pass it on to a friend, and share the contagious excitement of being *Ordinary Christians in a High-Tech World.*

ROBERT E. SLOCUM

ORDINARY CHRISTIANS IN A HIGH-TECH WORLD

WITH STUDY GUIDE FOR DISCUSSION AND REFLECTION

WORD BOOKS
PUBLISHER
WACO, TEXAS

A DIVISION OF
WORD, INCORPORATED

ORDINARY CHRISTIANS IN A HIGH-TECH WORLD

Library of Congress Cataloging in Publication Data:

Slocum, Robert E., 1938–
  Ordinary Christians in a high-tech world.

  1. Christian life—1960– .   2. Slocum, Robert E.,
1938– .   I. Title.
BV4501.2.S477   1986   261.1   86–1705
ISBN 0–8499–3046–4

Printed in the United States of America

6 7 8 9 8   MP   9 8 7 6 5 4 3 2 1

This book is dedicated to the monks at Arborcrest Abbey.

Thank God for Linda and Paul.

Contents

Preface

This book is written by a layman for the laity—for "ordinary Christians," not "Christian professionals" such as preachers and professors. I am writing about the role of lay men and women in the church at a particular time in history I call the "age of high technology"—a period that began in the middle of the twentieth century and is sweeping on into the twenty-first.

Clearly, the age of high technology is not just the wave of the future—it's here now! What does it mean to follow Jesus Christ in such a time? I attempt to answer this question from a lay perspective.

My choice to speak directly to the "person in the pew" does not reflect an anticlergy bias. As the saying goes, some of my best friends are ministers. And I welcome my clergy friends to look over some layperson's shoulder and join this discussion of the ordinary Christian's role in shaping the church's future.

At the same time, I have found that lay men and women are often far more aggressive than clergy and other church professionals in exploring a new future for the church, primarily because they are more acutely aware of the deficiencies of the church in those arenas where they live and work. In addressing the laity, I have no concept of "speaking down" to a spiritually or theologically inferior group of Christians! In fact, I have been tempted to rate the book "SML"—suitable for mature laity only—which means that clergy can be admitted only if accompanied by a layperson.

I am writing from the perspective of a layman in one of the "mainline churches" which has an ordained clergy. However, I am well aware that there is an important stream of Christian tradition—denominations, congregations, and parachurch movements—that relies primarily on lay leadership. One of the earliest examples of this in America was the Puritan congregation at Plymouth Plantation, which from 1620 to 1635 did nicely under the teaching of Elder William Brewster and survived four disastrous attempts to hire a professional minister or pastor.

But I believe that even in these traditions there is a tendency to place the emphasis of ministry on a few "special" individuals or to concentrate only on "church issues" and neglect the church's mission "out in the world." So I would urge Christians from *all* traditions to consider the issues raised here, even if the specific terminology I use and the church structures to which I refer are different from your own.

I begin this book by describing the laity, the church, and the high-tech age as I see them in the last decades of the twentieth century. My purpose in doing this is to set the stage for some creative dreaming about how equipped, enabled, and mobilized lay men and women can Christianize the age of high technology.

But making dreams a reality calls for strategy, and so the rest of the book centers on the idea of a personal strategy for each layperson. In parts 2 and 3, I suggest both an *interior* strategy and an *exterior* one. The interior strategy is based on the biblical concept of "HEART," which I explain fully in part 2. One of my own surprising discoveries in the preparation of the interior-strategy concept is the amazing power a developed, mature heart gives to the life of an ordinary Christian.

In part 3, I go on to explore an exterior strategy to guide each layperson in work, service, and ministry in the world and the church. Again, I invite my readers to join in the creative dreaming process in order to see the high-tech world around us through Christ's eyes. The key to effective lay ministry is a very clear understanding of Christ's call and a well-defined strategy that sets the priorities straight. The critical issue of support for lay ministry is also dealt with here.

Of the seven chapters that explore an exterior strategy,

only one chapter deals exclusively with the local congregation. This was unpremeditated but prophetic, since lay men and women spend only one-seventh or less of their week on the campus of their local congregation. Finding the balance between service and ministry in the "Church Gathered" as a local congregation and in the "Church Scattered" in the world is a major issue in plotting an external strategy.

I offer my readers two warnings. Both come from the fact that I am, by training and personality, a structural problem solver and entrepreneur.

First, my training and education is that of a scientist, engineer, and high-technology manager. My workday is filled with lasers, satellites, new company start-ups, and many such high-tech activities. Some readers may not understand this arena or even like people like me. (After seventeen years of marriage, my wife is still never quite sure what it is that I do for a living.) But in the arena of my daily work, I am still an ordinary layman trying to live out my Christian commitment. And I think my background gives me a unique perspective on how Christians can relate to the high-tech culture that is transforming our lives. So I hope you will be patient with the many examples and illustrations drawn from day-to-day events in my training and work. I will do my best to make them clear and meaningful.

The second warning is that my approach to the issues of lay ministry, like my approach to most things, is both structural and strategic. My entrepreneurial instincts force me to look at the church and ask, "What business are we in now? And what business *should* we be in for the high-tech age?" My creative dream for the church in the high-tech age calls for a new kind of structure that releases the people of God to impact the world for Jesus Christ. And this in turn requires a strategy, which is what I will be exploring throughout most of this book.

I do not pretend to present an exhaustive, detailed analysis of the age of high technology, a complete theology of the laity, or even a definitive statement on the status of

11

the church today. I have attempted to extract from these three areas the key interrelated issues and show practical ways they relate to the life of individual Christians. My prayer is that God can use my venture in structure and strategy to call ordinary Christians to greatly increased effectiveness in the church for the high-tech age.

Bob Slocum

Prologue:

The Mountain

It helps sometimes to think of God as a mountain.

This past September I was aboard an American Airlines flight from Dallas to Seattle. On the landing approach, as the plane dropped to twenty thousand feet, I heard people around me gasp. Through the window, I saw a gigantic mountain rising to meet us, looming a few thousand feet below the left wing tip. It was Mt. Rainier.

The day was crystal clear. The sunlight was blinding as it reflected off the crater at the summit, freshly filled by an early winter snowstorm. Every eye in the plane was fixed on Lady Rainier, with her ermine cape of twenty-three glaciers, sloping downward for nearly two vertical miles to the coastal plain.

My thoughts raced backward to a moment twenty years earlier when I stood on that summit. I had quit a job in Texas to come to Seattle and work for Boeing in space instrumentation. And before too long I would return to Texas. But before leaving the state of Washington I had given myself a very special going-away present—something I had been promising myself all year to do: I had climbed Mt. Rainier. Today, I am still amazed at how my personal encounter with God parallels my encounter with that mountain.

GLIMPSE OF A DISTANT PEAK

Texans believe that Texas is God's country, but after seeing the Pacific Northwest for the first time, I figured out where he takes his vacations! As I first drove into Seattle twenty years ago, rain and low fog hid the entire Cascade Range, Puget Sound, and the Olympic Mountains like a stage curtain. But the next morning the curtain lifted, and I was surrounded by snowcapped mountains and water. To someone who had lived exclusively on the plains of Oklahoma and Texas, the lone mountain rising more than fourteen thousand feet to punctuate the horizon one hundred miles to the southeast was truly spectacular.

I was amazed by the scene, but I soon noticed that the locals paid little attention to their distant scenic neighbor. They had grown used to it, and the thrill was gone.

This is how God seemed to me as I grew up in the Oklahoma wheat belt. I attended a Catholic school and the local Episcopal church, but to me God seemed hidden behind a curtain of liturgy and ritual. Then, at age twelve, I was baptized in the Disciples of Christ (Christian) Church, and the curtain opened. Like Mt. Rainier seen from Seattle, God seemed real but distant and unapproachable. As a teenager moving from the Southern Baptist to the Methodist to the Presbyterian churches, I noted that everyone seemed to believe that God was real, but no one seemed really to notice God in day-to-day life.

After September in Seattle, the sun and the mountain disappear into bleak, overcast winter. My first Seattle winter was a dreary and depressing one. But then one afternoon in the early spring, I noticed a strange lifting of spirits among my fellow employees at Boeing. I overheard someone telling his friend, "The mountain is out!" We gathered outside to find that the winter blanket of clouds had parted and Rainier had reappeared in the spring sunshine. People stood around staring at this first sign of spring.

For years God seemed like this to me—remote, hidden most of the time, but given to spectacular "pop-out" appearances. Sometimes, he would break through in a religious movie or book or during a moving Easter or Christmas service—intensely real for a fleeting moment. But then he would disappear again.

At Boeing, I worked beside several men who were

recreational fanatics, and each had a sort of inner clock that told him when time changed from sailing season to mountain climbing season, from skiing season to boat repairing season and back to sailing season. These coworkers worked with true missionary zeal to convert me into mountaineer and sailor.

A CLOSER LOOK AT THE MOUNTAIN

I finally joined them for a Saturday morning hike up Granite Peak, a mile-high hill by the side of the interstate. After several hours of huffing and puffing, we emerged above the timberline into a wonderland of July snowfields. I sat on a rock to eat my lunch and gaze at Mt. Rainier, free of clouds and three times closer and clearer than I had ever seen her before. The image burned slowly into my mind. I knew I would climb that mountain before I returned to Texas that fall.

In my spiritual pilgrimage, there have been several "hikes" similar to my Granite Peak experience—expeditions that have given me closer looks at God. For instance, two summers before high school graduation, I spent a week in the Ozark foothills at Dwight Mission, a former Cherokee mission school that the Presbyterians had converted into a conference center. I was so impressed with what I saw there that one day I hiked up into the hills overlooking the mission school grounds and prayed, "God, this Christian life looks great, and I want to get in on it. I don't know who Jesus Christ is, but whoever you say he is will be okay with me." The image of the God I saw that week was burned into my mind, just like the image of Mt. Rainier that I later saw from Granite Peak.

Once I made the decision to climb Mt. Rainier, I discovered there were rules and requirements. An inexperienced climber with no training must attend a climbing school that is approved by the National Park Service. I recruited two other friends for the climb—"Big John" from Montana and Roger from Kansas. We showed up at mile-high Paradise Lodge for climbing classes.

15

At Paradise Lodge, an experienced mountaineering guide introduced us to ropes for safety, an ice ax to brake sliding falls, and crampons for our boots with long metal spikes to grip the ice. The instructors taught us respect for the mountain by telling stories of a man who had fallen to his death off the end of a one-hundred-fifty-foot rope in the Tetons a month earlier and of a summer blizzard on the summit that had forced a climbing party into steam-heated ice caves for two days. We were given a personal look into a glacier and instructions for surviving a fall into a crevasse. A little mountaineering philosophy was thrown in: "It is not whether you get on top first that matters, but whether you get there at all."

"ARMCHAIR" MOUNTAIN CLIMBERS

While I waited for the week to pass before the actual climb, I announced my plans to my outdoor buddies at Boeing. And to my surprise, I discovered that some of these friends who had encouraged me to enjoy the "freedom of the hills" had *never climbed* Mt. Rainier! They had taken climbing classes, enjoyed the songs and the beer and the fellowship of the local climbing club. But they had never intended to set foot on this mountain for a personal encounter, because this climb took too much work and effort.

I can look back and see that many lay men and women I have known in churches seemingly stop short of a personal encounter with God. They show up regularly for the meetings, know all the songs, enjoy the fellowship, but they never actually "make the climb." Some of these people are the ones who have encouraged me on my own adventure of faith. But they have never abandoned their secure lives for an unreserved encounter with God.

My early experiences in the church led me to believe that only the professionals—the clergy—were supposed to go to the mountain for a personal encounter. But later, during the years I was studying engineering at the University of Oklahoma, I discovered a group of ordinary Christians who actually made the climb. They got together every Friday night so that people could tell stories of their personal encounters with God and how these encounters had changed their lives. The "climbers" who reported their experiences included fellow students, professors, businessmen and their wives, professional people, athletes, and even the former president of my social fraternity. Each person described the route he or she had followed to a personal encounter with Jesus Christ.

At these group meetings I was always treated well, encouraged to study the climbers' routes, listen to their stories, inspect all their climbing equipment, and of course make the climb myself. For several years, I continued to listen, to study, and to think over what I had heard, although it was a while before I actually was ready to commit myself to go on the Christian adventure.

CLIMB DAY!

Dawn appeared as a red-orange luminous glow behind the shadowy Cascade Range as we drove to join our climbing party at the Paradise Lodge Ranger Station. We covered the vertical mile to reach Camp Muir at ten thousand feet by sundown. I shivered till after midnight in my sleeping bag—too cold and tired to sleep. Shortly after midnight, we roped up and circled the rim of the Cowlitz Glacier, then scrambled up a steep rock wall. By sunup, we were halfway around the mountain and starting up the Emmons Glacier toward the summit. The pitch was so steep that steps had to be kicked in the ice for several thousand feet.

In the clear air I could see from Canada to California. But the climb was hard, painful work. Thirst on a mountain of ice, bursting lungs and aching legs, the searing sun, and the smell of wet leather and hemp are what I had paid my money for. I wanted to stop and, at times, to turn back. I discovered that sometimes the most difficult job in the world is putting one foot in front of the other, minute by minute, hour by hour.

My personal encounter with God paralleled my first encounter with the mountain. With all my research and careful study, I still underestimated the incredible experience of encountering the living Christ; I simply could not appreciate in advance the breathtaking view from the mountaintop. But I also underestimated the grinding discipline needed to put one foot in front of the other, to walk with Jesus Christ one day at a time. Both climbing and discipleship demand my full attention, stretch my resources to their limits, and force me to wonder, at times, if the rewards will be worth all the effort. But I made the decision when I started the climb that there would be no turning back.

In twenty-four sleepless hours on the mountain, I ascended nearly two vertical miles to the top of Mt. Rainier. The summit lay just behind a mysterious ridge that finally appeared at the headwall of the glacier. But a new surprise waited over that ridge. Rainier is a dormant volcano. The top is a shallow crater, dished out like a football stadium and filled with snow even in the summer. Once we were there, my body ached so badly that I couldn't even hike over to the crest of the rim and look out at the world (or let the world look at me). The summit held no *National Geographic* peak experience where I stood on the tip of a pinnacle rock to have my picture taken with flags of Texas and the United States fluttering from my ice ax. I was on top, but no one could see me, and I was unable to see out over the rim of the crater.

This mountain summit experience mirrors peak times in my pilgrimage with God. Most of my most important spiritual experiences have ended up going unnoticed in the eyes of the world. I find myself in the place God wants me to be, doing what God wants me to do. But no one seems to notice, and I don't have much of a view. God knows I am there and I know. But there are no color photos for *National Geographic*. All I have is the satisfaction of knowing that I have come a long, long way from the bottom with Jesus Christ and that I am where I am supposed to be.

THE TRIP DOWN

In mountaineering wisdom, the most dangerous part of any climb is the descent. Going up the mountain, my attention is riveted to the steps ahead while all my physical energy is consumed. A short rest on the summit unwinds my mind and relaxes my muscles. On the descent, however, gravity takes over and pounds my joints and muscles on every downward step. If I lose control or stumble, the trip down from the peak can be dangerous and even fatal.

The most dangerous times in my spiritual pilgrimage have also come after peak experiences. There is something about completing a task or reaching the goal that God called me to that causes me to relax mentally, physically, and spiritually. I feel I have it made, that nothing can happen because of what I have done with and for God. At times like these, if I'm not careful, I'm set up for a disaster.

On warm summer afternoons, the glaciers on Mt. Rainier begin to flow, opening and closing crevasses that block the route down from the summit. When crevasses must be jumped, each climbing group is roped together with a guide for safety. There was a guide shortage that weekend, and my group was assigned to a teenage recruit whom I charitably describe as a "jerk." He was inexperienced, undisciplined, always went too fast or too slow, and never seemed to know what was going on. He was easy to instantly dislike. On the descent, he and I were next to each other on the rope.

At each wide crevasse, the person behind would anchor the rope just in case the jumper failed to make the leap to the other side. But I had no intentions of falling; the thought of dangling for hours inside a glacier waiting for rescue tapped my unused energy reserves. On one leap, I cleared the crevasse with feet to spare, only to have the ice instantly give way and the sky disappear. I had overshot the landing spot and hit a snowbridge, a thin layer of snow that covers a hidden crevasse.

I opened my eyes and saw that I was dangling over the lip of the crevasse. My feet were walking on air. But the rope had held. My teenage partner—the jerk—had done his job exactly right and had checked my fall short of the depths of the crevasse. Climbing school instructions played like a tape in my mind. Roll over. Use ice ax as brake. Drive crampons into wall. I lunged as high up the wall as I could and

19

was able to drive my spikes into the ice. They held! I took another step with the other foot. They held! In moments, I was out and free, thanks to the flawless help of the teenage guide whom I had loved to hate.

PARTNERS IN THE CLIMB

On the mountain that day, I experienced the strange paradox of the freedom of the hills. The lure of the mountains is the call to face challenges of nature alone. Yet, the freedom to enjoy the hills often comes only when it is shared with partners. Freedom of the hills is achieved only when the hills can be enjoyed with safety and wisdom.

When I responded to the call to become personally involved with Jesus Christ, somewhere in the back of my mind was an image of a person alone on a great adventure with God. But, in reality, I find myself roped together with other members of God's family. Sometimes I am tied together with people I don't even like or enjoy being around. We are forced to learn to depend on each other as we jump the crevasses of day-to-day living. The trademark of the successful Christian expedition is effective roping together for the journey, not lonely isolation.

By early evening, the mountain was towering behind us, reflecting the fire and glow of a Pacific sunset. I made my way down through the high timber with the two friends I had recruited for the climb. We had made it to the top! The actual climb had taken more than thirty hours; I could almost feel the hot shower and taste a steak on the grill at the lodge just down the trail.

Then, without warning, one of my partners went down in the snow. Backtracking to where Roger was lying beside the trail, I bent over and listened to his words: "Just wanted to rest. Need a little sleep. Leave me alone. Go on and I'll be along later, after a little rest!"

We didn't know what to do. We weren't about to carry Roger, but we couldn't leave him in the subfreezing Rainier night. Then the climbing-school tape began to play again in my mind: "People sometimes give up, but at that point they can usually do twice as much as they have already done."

I prodded Roger and even gave him some gentle kicks and shoves. He drew up in a ball. I shook and kicked a little harder and he tried to defend himself. I began to put snow in his clothes and rub it in his face until he became so angry that he jumped to his feet and chased me. Then he stopped. We looked at each other and silently hiked on down to the lodge without further incident.

I have been on the Christian pilgrimage for more than twenty-five years. I am a little ashamed to admit it, but there are times when I feel that I have done all I can do and have gone as far as I am going to go. Why not let the others go on while I curl up in a snowbank tonight for a little rest? That is where other Christians come in. When I found the living Christ, he gave me the gift of brothers and sisters for the long journey. Occasionally, they must rub my face in the snow to get God's word through to me that I have the resources to go twice as far as I have already gone. Suddenly, I am on my feet again.

GATHERED AROUND THE FIRE

That evening, we treated blisters, sunburn, sore muscles, and the utter fatigue of thirty hours on the mountain without sleep. The expedition ended with a sizzling steak and a good night's sleep.

Why have I chosen this route to the summit of Mt. Rainier and back to begin a book about ordinary Christians in the high-tech age? One reason is that it brings us together around a bright, crackling fire in the majestic lodge at Paradise Valley on the flank of Mt. Rainier. This is the kind of place I would choose for this discussion—not a theology class-room or church building.

If I could gather around that fireplace with you, we would all soon realize that each person is at a different point in his or her own Christian pilgrimage. Some of you may have only viewed God from a distance. Some may have some-how caught a fleeting vision of God that captured their imaginations and compelled them to come further. Some may have been recruited by radio or TV evangelists or one of the effective parachurch groups such as Campus Crusade for Christ, Billy Graham, or Young Life. Those introduced to Christ in this way may have caught a ride to the mountain on a parachurch bus and will see the bus roll away as the real climb begins.

Some people are encountering the mountain for the first time as they begin the exciting, exhilarating ascent to the summit. At this moment, a few may be on a spiritual peak. Some may be dangling on a rope in a crevasse waiting and praying for rescue. Others may have served faithfully in their own congregation, putting one foot in front of the other year after year, without ever experiencing the excitement of seeing the clouds part to reveal the true Christian enterprise. Some may simply be worn out from the long climb and extended exposure and need rest and relaxation.

My goal is not to bunch people up at the same point along the trail. Regardless of where you are in your personal spiritual journey, my hope is that you will have the desire and openness to discover the next step God has for you and to find the courage to take that step. As I describe a mission for ordinary Christians in the high-tech age, I wish we could sit together before a blazing fire at a place like Paradise Lodge. But since we can't, I hope my words can free your imagination to dream creatively about your own "expedition" and the team of people who will ultimately join you in the climb.

A NEW MOUNTAIN

But here I want to change the image slightly. Not only is our experience of God something like climbing a mountain—so is our challenge as Christians in our world today. For I believe God is calling ordinary Christians like you and me to climb a *new* mountain. He is looking for men and women who will follow Jesus Christ into the age of high technology. In fact, I believe the entire church is being called to move forward into the high-tech age.

If this is a call for the whole church, why have I chosen to speak directly to the lay people instead of to the clergy? Because I predict it will be lay men and women who lead the climb into the high-tech age. The summit will be reached and conquered by ordinary men and women whose imaginations have been captured by Jesus Christ and who are empowered by his Spirit.

What about the learned theologians who staff theological seminaries? They can be compared to the people who know all about mountains. They are the geologists, geophysicists, volcanologists, and glaciologists who know all there is to know about rocks, mountains, volcanos, and glaciers. The clergy are the ones who run the mountaineering clubs and gather the club members every Sunday morning to hear mountaineering history and climbing stories. It is reported, however, that a disappointingly small number of climbing expeditions are launched by many of these clubs.

An uncomfortable question must be asked of the clergy and the current theologians: Who will prove to be the trustworthy guides for the laity? The absence of dynamic leadership for lay ministry in the past has sometimes been due to lack of experience and sometimes due to lack of commitment to the concept of "laity on the mountain" on the part of religious professionals. A major problem with many clergy and theologians is that they seem to prefer to stay with the same old territory. If I am correct that God is calling us to a new age and a new mission, church history predicts that the church professionals may be the last to respond.

I speak directly to the laity in this book because the laity make up more than 99 percent of the church. If God calls and ordinary Christians respond, congregations and denominational organizations will eventually follow. The laity must follow Jesus Christ into the age of high technology and, in the process, carry the church forward. If congregations fail to equip the laity and fail to support their mission, I believe the church as we know it will go out of business in the high-tech age.

A CHALLENGE TO CLIMB

It should be obvious that I am recruiting. I am looking for people called to this expedition to Christianize the high-tech age. Those who respond to this call—God's call—must know what they are doing. As they set out, they must ask a lot of difficult questions that demand answers if these people are to survive, eventually succeed, and be taken seriously by the church. They must take the challenge seriously.

In the next few chapters, I will be proposing that the church of Jesus Christ faces a major crisis in making a transition into the high-tech age. But I hope my readers will examine this proposal with a critical mind. Is it true that the institutional form of the church is so rooted where it is that it will resist moving forward into the high-tech age? And if so, what can and must be done about this resistance?

My personal conclusion is that the crisis faced by the church in the high-tech age is real and must be resolved by ordinary Christians. The task of Christianizing the high-tech age will fall squarely on the laity, not just on professional ministers, priests, and religious workers. What begins as a theoretical question about the church in the high-tech age and the laity in that church quickly moves beyond the theoretical to a personal, practical confrontation. *You,* my readers, are the answer to the problem—the solution to the crisis.

If the challenge is real and the call actually comes to you from God, what is the next step Christ would have you take? What will be required of you as an individual Christian when you respond to this challenge? These are the questions I hope will be foremost in your mind as the mountain rises ahead and you move forward for a closer look.

Part One

THE HIGH-TECH AGE, THE CHURCH— AND YOU!

1. Welcome to the High-Tech Age

A visit with my son, Paul, will introduce you to the high-tech age.

At eleven years of age, Paul recently acquired his own general-purpose computer—a Commodore 64 with 64K of memory. He already owned an Atari 2600 video game unit with 2K of memory. At last count, Paul had collected more than eighty video game cartridges on computer disks, cartridges, and cassettes (which he loads using the audio cassette recorder in his "boom box"). During his "BC" (Before Commodore) days, he found a keyboard for $3.95 in a bargain barrel, borrowed a BASIC cartridge from a junior-high-school student across the alley, and taught himself to program BASIC on his video game machine. Back then, he used the family TV for a display. But we are able to enjoy network programming again, because Paul now has a color monitor and the whole rig has been moved to his room. He does not interrupt his computer activities to watch TV, because he can record his favorite programs on a video recorder for later viewing.

Video games and computers are Paul's current hobby. He also has a keen interest in spiritual matters, and he especially likes C. S. Lewis's Narnia series of children's books and his science fantasy trilogy. But I worry that the church may become a low-tech relic from the past for Paul. What will he see and feel if he moves from his enriched world of high-tech sights, sounds, and interactive images into a Sunday school class that is run on conformity rather than creativity, cutouts and flannel boards rather than state-of-the-art electronic images, and dull teaching rather than participative learning?

I pray that Paul will not be a victim of a great crime against the gospel of Jesus Christ: making it boring! Millions of children like my son are true children of the high-tech age. Who can blame them for their lack of interest if they find themselves in a church that hides the Good News of Jesus Christ behind relics and rituals of an outmoded way of living?

THE HIGH-TECH AGE IS NOW

I have already stated that I believe the church is being called to follow Jesus Christ into the high-tech age. But what exactly do I mean by "high-tech age"?

I am referring to the current era in which we live—one in which the lives of ordinary people are impacted and even dominated by products, services, and experiences originating in the so-called high-tech industries. We know these industries by their products . . . electronics, computers, telecommunications, video and audio broadcasting and recording, biological and medical technology, space systems, lasers, exotic defense systems.

Many of us are high-tech workers whose daily work takes us to the soul of these industries each day. But the impact of the high-tech age is not limited to those who encounter it professionally; it is a pervasive force that penetrates the lives of all of us who live in the developed nations of the world.

The IRS has our life stories recorded in its massive computers. Word processors have invaded our offices and lasers print out our reports and letters with impressive clarity and speed. Images and sounds flood our homes with signals bounced from satellites or recorded on tapes and discs. Our taxes go toward elaborate computerized defense systems. Our bodies are examined, diagnosed, and treated by such complex equipment as sonograms, CAT scans, and microsurgery. Our children come home from school and tell us about their computer classes or head off to the local mall to play video games—if they don't have video games in their own living rooms.

THE WAVE OF THE FUTURE

A very helpful explanation of the high-tech age and the way it affects our lives is the one given by author Alvin Toffler in his book, *The Third Wave*.[1] Toffler describes the high-tech age as the most recent of three great trends or "waves" of change that have swept over the human race. Each wave introduced a new era for human civilization.

The "First Wave" as described by Toffler introduced agriculture. The simple acts of planting seeds and domesticating animals transformed a world of nomadic hunters and gatherers into one of settled farmers and ranchers. Communities sprang up, and the agricultural era had begun.

The "Second Wave" brought in the Industrial Revolution some three hundred years ago. After this wave passed, the world was divided into two groups: producers and consumers. No longer did each community produce only what it could consume. The world was quickly immersed in a sea of manufactured goods and products, along with the suggestion that we are duty-bound to consume, if possible, all that is offered. In time, all major "Second Wave" institutions such as banking, education, government, and manufacturing were organized around six basic principles or goals: centralization, maximization, concentration, synchronization, specialization, and standardization.[2]

The exact moment of the beginning of the "Third Wave"— what I call the high-tech age—is open to question, but it happened sometime in the 1950s. To describe this new wave and the impact it has made on civilization, Toffler focuses on four emerging industries: electronics (with the associated explosive growth in advanced communications and computers), the space industry, an industrial push into the

---

1. New York: Bantam, 1980.
2. Ibid.

oceans, and the business enterprise growing out of genetic engineering.

I remember exactly when the high-tech age started for me. I was sitting in an engineering physics class when the professor announced the Russian launching of Sputnik I, the first artificial satellite to orbit the earth. But looking back, I can see that the Third Wave was rolling in and affecting my life even before that.

I grew up in Canadian County, Oklahoma, which was the land area originally allotted to the Cheyenne and Arapaho tribes when Oklahoma was Indian Territory. These tribes had moved from nomadic life in Colorado and Wyoming into the First Wave (agriculture) and on into the Second Wave (industry) in a few generations. By the time I was born in 1938, the primary industries of El Reno, the county seat, were flour mills and a major repair yard for the railroad that hauled the wheat to market. My mother and father owned and operated the three movie theaters in the town. Then, in 1947, the precursor of the Third Wave arrived in El Reno—television! Business at our movie theaters deteriorated to the point that my parents gave up and moved to another city to find jobs. In my family, we were experiencing an economic depression resulting from a new high-tech industry.

It is only in looking back, however, that I can see the way the beginnings of the Third Wave affected my life. Sometimes it is difficult to sense the effect of radical change when we are riding a wave, carried along with the flow. This is probably true for most of us in the United States, where much of the high-tech wave is generated and experienced. Even though we talk about how quickly things are changing in our world—and we gape at the advances made by computers and other high-tech developments, I believe we fail to comprehend fully how sweeping the changes have been in our own lives.

It is often easier to grasp the impact of a new wave by observing its effect on someone else. This is what was done in a ground-breaking study made several decades ago in Mexico by Michael Maccoby and Eric Fromm.

WELCOME TO THE HIGH-TECH AGE

In 1961, Maccoby went to Mexico for psychoanalytic training under Fromm. Over an eight-year period, these two men observed changing patterns of hopes, attitudes, and dreams in both the quiet villages and one of the world's great metropolitan areas, Mexico City.

Fromm and Maccoby conducted a systematic investigation of the work and character of the simple villagers.[3] As these trained psychologists examined the fabric of traditional rural society, which for centuries had been run by small land owners, they made a surprising discovery. A quiet revolution was taking place in the Mexican culture, as new work methods and new products created by American corporations visibly reshaped the attitudes and goals of workers.

Even in rural villages nothing had greater impact on the lives of people than high-technology products from the United States. The arrival of complex farm machinery, electronics, chemicals, TV, radio, and modern marketing techniques was calling forth a new breed of high-tech workers who suddenly found themselves in positions of leadership. The Third Wave was rolling in, and the changes were more dramatic in the areas where it was rolling into an essentially First Wave culture.

Looking back, I can see now the gradual impact of the Third Wave on my hometown in Oklahoma. I can speculate on changes in traditional lifestyles when the homes of Mexico City are wired for cable TV and are instantaneously flooded with American network programs and commercials. I can picture people in a remote Mexican village clustered around a TV set when the communication satellite is first switched on. What I cannot see clearly is what is happening to me and to my own family as the high-tech wave rolls over us. Yet in all of these cases the question is the same. How do I react and respond to this Third Wave—this age of high technology—which is transforming my work, family life, and social structure?

---

3. Eric Fromm and Michael Maccoby, *Social Character in a Mexican Village* (Englewood Cliffs, NJ: Prentice-Hall, 1970).

I am a technologist and have actually worked professionally in three of the four areas Toffler pinpoints to describe the Third Wave. I have seen firsthand some of the amazing developments that have taken and are taking place in the high-tech age. But in this chapter I will refrain from making my own predictions and pronouncements about the achievements of modern science in order to consider how the high-tech age affects the church—especially ordinary Christians in the church—and how I believe the church must respond to the changes taking place around it.

THE CHURCH AND THE HIGH-TECH WAVE

For over thirty years now, the wave of the high-tech age has been rolling in, gradually sweeping over the billion people in the developed nations of the world. Whether we like it or not, and whether we are ready or not, the wave is a reality. The church may fail to get the word or feel that it is a fortress on a hill, safely resting far above the high-tide line. But the ordinary Christians out in the world are being carried along by the high-tech tidal wave and must sink or swim.

Even though the Third Wave is flooding the world around us, some laity find that they are a part of congregations that have not even experienced the Second Wave! The pastor and the congregation still function in mode of the First Wave village church in an agricultural community. The pastor or priest is the local holy man and guru on religious matters, and the laity are not expected to know anything of the lofty matters of theology and religion. The villagers depend on the pastor for spiritual services in the same way that they depend on the village lawyer for legal services and the village doctor for medical services. There is no intention of educating the villagers in the matters of law, medicine, or theology.

Most congregations, however, have been dragged—perhaps kicking and screaming—into the era of the Second Wave—the Industrial Revolution. After its first three hundred years, the church assumed an institutional form that entails professional staffs, buildings, lands, and seminaries. The "Second Wave" institutional church has fallen in line with other institutions such as banking, education, government, and manufacturing in aggressively pursuing the Second Wave goals of centralization, maximization, concentration, synchronization, specialization, and standardization. The trouble is that while industry and other institutions are abandoning these six Second Wave goals as they move into the high-tech age, the church for the most part has failed to follow along and seek a new path.

For lay men and women who are daily swept along by the Third Wave out in their world between Sundays, it is very important to recognize a congregation that is stuck in the Second Wave era. It falls to the laity to break the church loose to move into the high-tech age. The key issues for the church will arise from the six characteristic goals of Second Wave institutions, which must be rethought and revised for Third Wave effectiveness.

The first issue is centralization. Industries of the Second Wave operated on the assumption that pulling everything together at one central location was the way to go. The Second Wave congregation operates on the same principle—pulling people together at a central location so that the main activities of the church can revolve around what happens on campus in the church buildings.

Today, however, industry is learning that improved productivity and labor-management relations are achieved in plants with hundreds, not thousands, of workers. Workers are increasingly productive in small teams, not on endless assembly lines. The computer industry—a banner industry of the high-tech age—has moved quickly from the time of the gigantic central computer to decentralized personal computers.

In the same way, the Third Wave church will need to focus on decentralized teams of equipped laity as the church in the world instead of concentrating all activities on Sundays at the sanctuary. The decentralized church that is meeting in small groups and classes in homes, businesses, and offices around the city or community will be the springboard for ministry in the high-tech world. The impact of a decentralized church will be unbelievably great when compared with that of Second Wave churches holding to the idea that *the* church is exclusively the church gathered in one central location.

The second issue is maximization. Second Wave churches tend to be preoccupied with numbers and the question of how big they can become (or how small they have become). And no one can appreciate the "bigness is greatness" philosophy any better than a Texan like myself. I catch myself telling people that I am an elder in the largest Presbyterian church in the United States. But so what? Isn't it much more important to be an elder in the most *effective* Presbyterian church in the United States—regardless of size?

Industry is discovering that there are optimum sizes for greatest effectiveness—and that biggest is not always best! Third Wave companies, such as the 3M Corporation, now restrict the size of business units to achieve maximum effectiveness. Similarly, a Third Wave church is one that learns to abandon maximization as a goal and to concentrate on optimization. The question for every congregation and group within the congregation must be: What is the optimum size that will enable us to be most effective in the tasks to which God calls us?

Concentration is the third issue. Second Wave industries concentrated power almost exclusively in the hands of owners and high-ranking executives. Third Wave companies are pushing ownership and management participation to the lowest levels of the corporate family with amazing results. But Second Wave churches remain committed to concentrating all power and control in the hands of senior clergy, their hand-picked staff, and very select lay leaders. A Third Wave church recognizes that each member who knows the indwelling Christ is a gifted individual and potential leader. I firmly believe that the distribution of power and leadership responsibilities among the people of God who are ministering and growing through small group experiences will lead to an explosive emergence of leadership talent.

A peculiar quirk of the Second Wave culture is synchronization, the requirement to get all people to do things at the same time. The invention of the factory forced large groups of people to get up at the same time, to drive the freeways at the same time, to sleep at the same time, and to be entertained at the same time. The Second Wave church has also tended to make a fetish of synchronization. When classrooms or the sanctuary are filled two hours per week, we build new, larger buildings rather than change the times of meetings to meet the demand.

Third Wave industries are moving toward flextime, which allows workers to select their hours and even their worksite. I believe the Third Wave church will adopt a similar philosophy, asking what is the best time for effective ministry and utilization of available resources. In Seattle, where life is oriented around outdoor recreation and 7 percent of the people attend church, I would expect the approach to be quite different from that in Dallas, where attending church is a popular social outing.

The fifth issue is specialization. This can be described as the tendency to know more and more about less and less until you know everything about nothing. American business is now realizing that it has been stung by "specialist" strategic planners who sit in remote offices and write strategic business plans for the corporation. As these specialists have led company after company into disasters, it has become clear that, given the training and tools, the operating managers who best know the business are the ones who write the best strategic plans.

The Second Wave church is deep into specialization— with equally harmful results. Those who have specialized seminary training are assumed to know the most about God and his people. I recall my own amazement recently at visiting a Sunday school class attended by some of the brightest, most capable young leaders in the city. These young men and women truly believed that no one *in* the class could *teach* it! They felt that only someone from their church staff could teach the class. The Second Wave church will hire professional psychological counselors while totally ignoring the healing power of lay-led small group counseling as pioneered by Alcoholics Anonymous. The Third Wave church is one that bets heavily on the emerging gifts in lay ministry teams and small groups to augment or to replace the work of specialized professionals.

A final issue is standardization. Second Wave industry carried standardization to extremes in everything from automobiles to hamburgers because of the economy of making the same thing over and over. The Third Wave industries are breaking this trend and heading in the direction of customization. Computer-controlled manufacturing processes make it just as simple to produce custom integrated circuits or machine parts as it is to make them all the same.

The Second Wave church has made standardization and sameness its trademark. Within each denomination and congregation, the preaching, music, and teaching tend to be standardized and more or less the same week after week. This sameness permeates denominations so that it is almost possible to walk into a sanctuary on any Sunday morning and guess the group's affiliation. The Third Wave church is one that recognizes the diverse needs for worship experiences, teaching, preaching, and outlets for lay mission within each individual congregation and develops a customized response in each major area.

THE ROLE OF THE ORDINARY CHRISTIAN

What is the role of the ordinary Christian in all of this? No amount of scrutiny of the Second Wave church will produce a final answer—although understanding it can help. Nor will the answer be found in a simple evaluation of the "gee whiz" features of the Third Wave world around us. But I believe a key to the answer can be found in an understanding of waves themselves.

The great "rollers" that pound the beaches along the Northern Pacific coast of Mexico are waves that I have studied personally. I can sit under a thatched roof shelter for an hour at the most before the irresistible urge to enter the surf seizes me. I wade out to where the foaming breakers blow to the sky and the blue-green wall of water rolls over me. As I flip end over end, salt water is pumped into every hole in my head. After being dragged back and forth in the undertow until my swimsuit fills with sand, I am dumped on the beach. I tell myself that this is great fun. It is also the style of lay ministry in the high-tech age.

The laity must sense the high-tech wave rising and hear a call to follow Jesus Christ in the rising tide. They cannot afford to wait on a church stuck in the First Wave or Second Wave cultures and unable or unwilling to change. The role of ordinary Christians is to carry the church into the high-tech world where they already live and work.

To do this, lay men and women must be equipped to survive, as well as to minister. But who *are* the laity? What is their role in the individual congregation, the church, the world? And how can they be renewed and empowered to carry out the crucial work of Christ in the world? In the next chapter, I hope to point toward some possible answers.

2. Who Is the Church?

Show me your church![1]

The request is always welcome, but my problem is selecting an appropriate response. If I am in a creative mood and prone to think big, we could catch a flight to Orlando, Florida, drive out to Cape Canaveral, and board a space shuttle. As we silently orbit the earth, I could turn one of the Space Telescopes toward the land surfaces and point out the people of God scattered throughout towns, cities, and countrysides in each country on every continent. This is my church, the "Church Universal."

If I am in a more nationalistic mood, I could set up meetings at our denominational headquarters in Atlanta and New York for an overview of the recently reunited Presbyterian Church (USA). This is my "Denominational Church." Or we might visit a Young Life club on a high school campus or a Campus Crusade meeting on a university campus. Here, we could see the dynamic effect of these campus ministries that make up my "Parachurch."

If this request came from an early riser, we could visit a breakfast group where people meet before work for prayer, sharing, and Bible study. At this meeting, we would see

1. In this chapter, I will be talking about church renewal. Not everyone feels this is an issue in their church. Last summer I visited with a national leader of a large Pentecostal denomination. He explained that there was no renewal movement in his denomination because they considered themselves to be a renewed church. I periodically meet members of new evangelical "start-up" congregations who believe they have found the elusive formula for dynamic congregational life and ministry. Readers who feel they belong to an ideal congregation in which renewal is not an issue may want to skip this chapter and continue with part 2. On the other hand, they may find that reading it helps them understand some of the issues with which other congregations struggle.

men and women who are attempting to follow Christ in the world "between Sundays." These are my partners in what I call the "Church Scattered."

All of these threads are part of the fabric that is the church. But the odds are that my response to someone who wanted to see my church would be the same predictable response of most lay people: "Great! What are you doing Sunday morning?" Mention "my church" and the first thing that usually pops into my mind is the local congregation where I am a member. This is the "Church Gathered," the place where members come together each week for worship, preaching, teaching, fellowship, and participation in whatever projects and ministries the congregation has elected to sponsor.

Meet me next Sunday morning in the affluent Highland Park neighborhood of Dallas and, if you can find a place to park, I will give you the tour. We can admire the stately Gothic buildings, set among towering old pecan trees. When the sound of the organ and choir begins, we can find a seat in the sanctuary to hear the sermon. Later, we can visit a church school class, and I will introduce you to some of the officers, staff, and members.

No matter what the town or the city or the size of the congregation or extent of the facilities, each layperson could conduct a tour of this type. Some tours may take longer than others. But for most Christians, "my church" means the Church Gathered, the congregation who meet "on site" at the regularly appointed hour. Even with the rise of parachurch organizations, radio and TV evangelists, and ecumenical projects, the age of high technology opens with the laity clustered around local congregations where they are members.

WHO ARE THE LAITY?

Although I am a layman, I usually think of myself first of all as a member of my congregation. I belong to the church and I normally give little thought to the fact that I belong to a specific segment of the church called the laity. For those of us who are the laity, there tends to be little group identity and little sense of belonging to the laity. This is not surprising since the laity are normally defined in terms of what they are *not*. The laity are not clergy, preachers, priests, or ordained members of religious orders. But who are they? And what is their role in the church?

In the twentieth century, the question has become even more complicated. As Christianity has become not only an institution, but also an enterprise, tens of thousands of people have gone to work for religious foundations, church and parachurch organizations, religious counseling centers, and businesses specializing in religious music, broadcasting, and publishing. Such people fall in a grey area; they are what I call "clericalized laity." Even though they are not ordained seminary graduates, they do draw a paycheck for professional religious work.

Do the clericalized laity fit in best with the clergy or the mainstream laity? I have found that such people normally tend to develop the mindset and mental outlook of whoever signs their paycheck. In addition, they receive positive strokes from the clergy, who regard them as the "good laity" because of their full-time religious work. And so the clericalized laity tend to be pulled into the camp of the clergy and professional religious workers, and this sets them apart from ordinary laity. This is not a judgment of the vocational calling of the clericalized laity. But such a calling may make it more difficult for them to develop a fresh vision of the call and the mission of ordinary lay people.

Several years ago, I served on a team planning the Presbyterian Congress on Renewal held in January 1985. As we put together the program, I pointed out the need for a forum on the role of the laity in the Presbyterian Church for the future. I was immediately confronted by two good friends, both Presbyterian ministers, who charged that I was just campaigning for my own special interest group. For an instant I was shocked and angry. When I recovered my sense of humor, I pointed out that a group that makes up at least 98 percent of the church hardly constitutes a special interest group! At the next meeting (from which I happened to be absent), my two friends saw to it that such a forum on the laity was included in the official schedule.

Because congregational activities normally revolve around the clergy, both laity and clergy seem unaware that the laity constitute at least 98 percent of the church. And few seem to recognize that this number can be further divided along the practical lines of what I call "churchy" laity and "worldly" laity. I mean *nothing derogatory* by either term. The "churchy" laity invest time and energy in their congregation, keeping the Church Gathered running smoothly. They can be found teaching classes, raising and counting money, serving on boards and committees, serving communion, and even preaching on Laymen's Sunday. They help the clergy do their jobs.

In a typical congregation, all the job openings for "churchy" laity can be filled by less than 20 percent of the congregation. The "worldly" laity make up the remaining 80 percent, who focus their time and energy out in the world from Monday morning until Saturday night. They are at their stations in factories, corporations, professional offices, homes, schools, workshops, banks, government agencies, stores, and hundreds of other workplaces beyond the church grounds. Whether they know it or not, the "worldly" laity are the people of God in the world.[2]

I believe that each of us, whether we are "churchy" laity or "worldly" laity, must take a critical look at our relationship with our congregations. Whenever I envision the laity in most churches I have encountered, my mental image is of men and women loosely clustered together in a congregation, usually with a vague uncertainty as to exactly what is expected of them as Christians in a changing world. And I am convinced this must change if the church is to remain vital in the high-tech age.

When Christ chooses one of us out of the crowd for a

---

2. I owe this concept of "churchy" laity and "worldly" laity to Mark Gibbs and T. Ralph Morton, who introduced it in their book, *God's Frozen People* (Philadelphia: Westminster, 1964). Type "A" laity ("worldly") have their main interests in the world outside the church buildings. Type "B" laity ("churchy") find the main interest of their life centers on their church and its activities. Both are important, and many of us have mixed (A and B) roles.

specific mission, our first reaction is to look to our congregation for support. There is nothing wrong with this; it is the way the church is supposed to function. But when it comes to being Christ's people in the high-tech age, survival demands that we learn to "read" our congregations to determine what we can realistically expect in the way of practical support and help. The suggestion that we are about to enter a new age and must define a new role and new mission for the laity is enough to give some congregations a nervous breakdown. It is an unpleasant truth that many congregations are in no way prepared to support lay ministry and mission in the high-tech age or any other age.

Congregations are categorized in a variety of insightful ways by church historians and sociologists. For my purposes, the most useful descriptions would be those my readers would give me if we could actually sit down together around the campfire. How would you describe the way your congregation functions? What is the role of the laity? My experience tells me your descriptions would run the gamut from what I call "caretaker congregations" to "renewal congregations" that focus sharply on lay ministry.

CARETAKER CONGREGATIONS

In the caretaker model, traditional priests or clergy are called to oversee a passive flock of laity. In the very worst scenario, the caretaker clergy expect three things. They expect the laity to show up, to put up, and to shut up. The laity, in turn, also expect three things. They expect their pastor to dress like a pastor; they expect their church building to look like a church; and they expect to be left alone. I will add an expectation of my own. I expect the caretaker congregations to go out of business in the high-tech age. I predict that their seven last words will be, "We never did it this way before!"

From a lay ministry perspective, the caretaker congregation is of little help at best and is a dangerous obstacle at worst. Unfortunately, the caretaker model is deeply entrenched in North America and Europe. This is the starting point for millions of lay men and women who begin their climb in response to a personal call from Jesus Christ. The caretaker model calls for a static, motionless laity. The dynamic role of the laity that I believe is essential for the success of the church in the high-tech age is truly incomprehensible to a caretaker congregation.

From the perspective of the caretaker congregation, any layperson with enough gifts and spiritual energy to even consider a serious mission for God would be expected to channel it into something "useful" like going to seminary and getting ordained. If Christ calls me to follow him in a new way in this high-tech age, my caretaker congregation may not support me or even understand. There is a possibility that I may even be totally abandoned in my new venture of discipleship.

To return to the image of mountain climbing, when God calls me to mission and ministry in the high-tech age, I need a training camp where I can learn from experienced climbers, develop my own skills, get in shape, and develop as part of a team with others who are called to join with me. When I actually venture on the mountain and launch out to assault the summit, I need a base camp. The base camp must provide shelter from the storm, a place to rest, storage for supplies, and a place for fellowship and strategy with the rest of the climbing party. My partners at the base camp are the ones who will look for me if I set out for the summit and do not return.

Is it realistic to expect a congregation to function as both training camp and base camp for lay mission and ministry? It seems unlikely that caretaker congregations can perform this function. But what about "renewal congregations"? The situation is more encouraging in these churches, but there are still problems. (My purpose here is not to criticize specific congregations or movements, but rather to encourage my fellow laypeople to make an accurate assessment of the conditions, attitudes, and capabilities of their own congregations.)

TOE-IN-THE-WATER RENEWAL

I have been a part of the church renewal movement in the United States for nearly thirty years. The most common type of congregation I have worked with is one *considering* the need for renewal and lay ministry. These churches are willing to put at least one toe in the water and experiment, even if they don't feel ready to plunge wholeheartedly into the waters of renewal.

As I have observed toe-in-the-water renewal congregations around the country, I have found a strange paradox. These renewal congregations frequently promise far more than they are able to deliver as far as the laity are concerned. New life is breaking out in these congregations as people open their lives to Jesus Christ. But although personal renewal is taking place, the direction in which congregations are headed is unchanged and still leaves the laity unsupported for following Christ in the high-tech age. Personal renewal generates a tremendous outburst of hope, but the expected support from the congregation fails to materialize.

I first noticed this phenomenon as I led lay renewal conferences in Presbyterian congregations. I found tremendous hope and excitement in these congregations as we held weekend renewal conferences. Lay witness teams were invited into the church to share how God was working in their lives. As members of the congregation listened to the teams, they would open up and share their own experiences. During the conferences, God moved in new ways to draw people to Jesus Christ and transform relationships. These were exciting times when the love of God was felt in a fresh, dynamic way within the congregation.

But then a year or so passed and calls began to come from people who wanted a second conference to "pump up" the congregation. As I visited these congregations, I would discover a handful of people, touched deeply by God in the first conference, now huddled together over embers of dying renewal fires in a remote corner of the sanctuary. Meanwhile, the church was back to business as usual. The old programs rolled on as if nothing had happened.

44

These toe-in-the-water congregations offered people a renewal experience, but the offer expired when the weekend was over. The people whose lives had been touched by Christ had honest expectations of a continuing renewal community that would love, accept, and care for them as they lived out their new commitments to Christ. But congregations were not delivering what they had unwittingly promised. And unfulfilled hopes for renewal of the church were grinding people up. For many lay men and women, the touch of Christ had been real, but the inability of the congregation to function as a caring, supportive family left them with the mixed feelings of having been blessed and "ripped off" at the same time.

It took me a while to find the root of the problem, but finally I saw why many of these laypeople were so frustrated and disappointed. We were not doing *church* renewal conferences at all; we were doing *personal* renewal conferences in a congregational setting. And we were doing nothing to change the basic structure and operation of the congregations. So the tendency after a special time of renewal was simply to roll back into the old ways of doing things.

When I finally realized how widespread this problem was in churches, I became very discouraged. It looked like a hopeless situation to me. In many congregations I visited, the pastors and most of the lay people seemed perfectly content with the way things were. Their attitude seemed to be that a little renewal was okay as long as you don't overdo it. Perhaps I overreacted, but eventually I became so depressed over the situation that I gave up leading renewal conferences in congregations.

But then one weekend I made plans to fly to Washington, D.C., to attend a national conference for seminary students and professors. Getting on the plane, I discovered Dr. Robert Munger, who was headed to the same meeting. Dr. Munger was then professor of evangelism at Fuller Seminary and a leader of seminary student teams that held congregational renewal conferences. Bob had been a true spiritual guide for me over the years. I dropped into a seat beside him, and I'm sure my discouragement showed. I decided to test my ideas about the "great renewal rip-off." Here was my chance to find out if I was wrong.

Bob listened attentively as I told my story. Then he finally asked, "Do you know any church that has it together?" I risked exposing my own limited knowledge by giving him an honest answer. "No, I really do not." He then pinned me down a little tighter by asking, "What about —— Church?" (He named an outstanding congregation with an excellent staff.) "Do you think they have it together?"

I took a deep breath. I had never met the prominent senior minister or visited the church, and I felt a twinge of fear that a critical comment might get back to them. But some of my friends attended there, so I had an answer that I shared with a good deal of hesitation. "No, Dr. Munger, I don't believe they have it together."

STAFF-CENTERED RENEWAL

To my surprise, Bob smiled and assured me I was right. He went on to explain why. The church had an outstanding preacher, an excellent staff, and fine programs. When all these "generals" paraded, the "privates" (the laity) gathered to watch and applaud. The problem was that none of the troops knew how to march! That was because there were no "sergeants" or "lieutenants." In other words, the problem in that church was a lack of leadership to train and equip the laity.

Dr. Munger's analysis helped me to see that, from a lay perspective, church-staff-led renewal is only one step beyond toe-in-the-water renewal. Of course, I celebrate whenever any kind of renewal breaks out, and I know that clergy and staff leadership is essential for the authentic renewal of a congregation. But I believe the determining factor in whether a congregation is able to move successfully into the high-tech age is whether or not the "troops" can "march." And I am convinced this requires a church emphasis on ministry of the laity—not on ministry of the church staff.

What about congregations that appear to be very successful yet have as their primary focus the ministry of the church staff? When I was doing graduate work in physics, my fellow students had a saying about the math graduate school, at the same university: "Get a Ph.D. in math here and be one of the great mathematicians of the 1930s!" In other words, you would be well-trained but forty years behind the times! In the same way, I believe a congregation built on the idea of putting the staff and clergy on parade rather than putting the laity on the firing line can still become one of the great churches of the 1940s or 1950s but certainly not of the high-tech age.

During the past year, I had an exciting opportunity to work with the elders of the University Presbyterian Church in Seattle at their annual retreat. The leader of this team of elders, Senior Minister Bruce Larson, expressed his concern that this established congregation, which has been experiencing vital new growth and success, could nevertheless become a "great, mediocre church." As I visited with Bruce, he shared his goal that the church should not just *appear* to be doing great in comparison with other congregations in the Seattle area or even the entire Presbyterian denomination. Bruce was concerned that the congregation reach its full potential as the people of God. Anything less is mediocre regardless of the apparent outward success.

In the high-tech age, a simple model of a "great, mediocre church" is a football game. The center of attention in the game is twenty-two people on the stadium floor in desperate need of rest. The stadium seats are filled with seventy thousand people in desperate need of exercise.

A GREAT, GREAT CHURCH

The great, mediocre churches are those doggedly locked in on the ministry of the staff and clergy. I believe the "great, great" congregations of the high-tech age will not be judged on size, growth rate, or the number of spiritual all-stars on their payroll. The "great, great" churches will be those that serve as training camps and base camps for lay men and women who hear Christ call them to climb their particular mountain and who respond to that call.

A new strategy for the church in the high-tech age will

47

make three demands of the laity. First, we must become equipped and enabled so that we not only survive but also minister in the world of the high-tech age. Second, we must assume, if necessary, the responsibility for our own equipping. Third, the church must be carried forward into the high-tech age, and the laity must assume responsibility for this task. If this third task is left to the religious professionals, there is a distinct possibility that the church as we know it faces extinction in the high-tech age.

At this point in history, all laypersons must make an honest evaluation of the help that can realistically be expected from their own church and congregation when they set out to be the people of God in the world where God has placed them. It is a fair criticism of the state of the church in this century that it has failed time after time to recognize and support the call of the laity to ministry. Whatever other successes the church has achieved in North America and Europe, it has failed on a grand scale to equip and mobilize the laity for ministry.

Now, the picture isn't entirely bleak. European students of lay ministry look upon the millions of Americans involved in Sunday school programs as a major accomplishment in the ministry of the laity. Many of the church's ministries and programs are of direct or indirect value to ordinary Christians. Pockets of renewal keep appearing in evangelical, Pentecostal, and Catholic—as well as mainline—congregations across the country. And there *are* congregations that are focusing on ministry of the laity rather than on ministry of the staff. The laity who find these equipping and support centers come away with exciting reports of being freed, outfitted, and turned loose to be about the life and ministry to which God calls them. Such renewal congregations, which are lay ministry centered, are inspiring prototypes of the church for the high-tech age.

But the number is still disappointingly small. I believe the church must be encouraged and praised when it does provide effective support for the laity and their mission. But the church must be confronted and challenged to true renewal when it fails to take the mission and ministry of the laity seriously.

WHO IS THE CHURCH?

Last month at the Presbyterian Congress on Renewal in Dallas, I asked the participants in my seminar to evaluate their congregations with respect to lay ministry. One third of the group was clergy and the rest were laity. They were asked to pick a number based on "0" for a pure caretaker congregation, "5" for toe-in-the-water renewal, "8" for staff-led renewal, and "10" for lay-ministry-centered renewal. The average score for the thirty-five congregations represented was "4½"—not quite toe-in-the-water status.

But no matter what the state of the church, as ordinary Christians we face the challenge to follow Jesus Christ into the high-tech age. When God speaks to us in a personal call to obedience, we can't decline with the excuse that our individual congregation isn't up to it just yet.

We hear and we must respond, even if it means setting out on a journey that our church or our minister may not understand or support. It can be a lonely and frightening journey if we go alone. We need and must pray for partners who are also called by God—people who can celebrate with us the call to the high country and the encounter with the mountain.

LOOKING AHEAD

It is clear that the emergence of a church for the high-tech age will not just happen. Effective lay leadership will not come about without a strategy. What strategy will allow this to happen? Those who hold tenaciously to the Second Wave model of the church will be skeptical of any strategy that does not originate with professional clergy. I believe the most promising strategy for the high-tech age will be the personal strategy developed by each layperson in response to a personal call to ministry from Jesus Christ. Such a strategy will include an inventory of aptitudes and spiritual gifts that must be invested for Christ as an act of intelligent stewardship. A Third Wave congregation must develop its strategy for ministry around the spiritual gifts and calls of the ordinary Christians who are its members.

Even if the congregations and denominations choose to

49

stay behind, the laity must implement their personal strategies for ministry. An effective personal strategy is made up of two parts, an interior strategy and an exterior strategy. In part 2 of this book, I will explore an interior strategy based on the idea that the interior life centers on the five dimensions of the heart. The interior strategy calls for a systematic development of the biblical heart to achieve maturity in each of the five dimensions. I will describe this process and explore the surprising differences between the biblical concept of HEART and the usual concepts that occur in ordinary conversations and literature. A developed heart is a long-term goal for anyone who will follow Jesus Christ into the high-tech age.

Ministry, work, and service in the high-tech age are charted by an external strategy. Each layperson must develop an external strategy that covers the arenas of work, marriage, government, and the church. We must work to clarify Christ's call to service and ministry in each of these four areas. As the high-tech wave rolls in and shifts the sand and moves the rocks, a clear, workable strategy is needed even for survival—not to mention an effective lay ministry.

In part 3, I will explore each of these four major arenas of an exterior strategy. Because the Second Wave church is in the habit of acting as if the Church Gathered is the only church that matters, I will discuss the Church Gathered and Church Scattered in separate chapters. "Church Scattered" describes the people of God from the time they leave the sanctuary on Sunday morning until they return the next week. I am convinced that the Church Scattered will steadily climb to new heights of importance in the high-tech age because this is where the people of God encounter the high-tech world.

All that is missing from the overall personal strategy is the pin that securely links the interior strategy with the exterior strategy. The emerging answer is the small group—people who are linked together to develop and implement their own personal strategies in responsible obedience to Jesus Christ. A group like this is a laboratory for the heart and provides a continual challenge to work toward maturity and growth of the heart. The group must also provide ongoing help for identification and clarification of ministry in new and uncharted territory. When the heart is severely tested in the arenas of the exterior strategy, this group must provide support, affirmation, and empowerment in Christ's name while holding each person accountable for obedience to Christ's call.

An interior strategy and an exterior strategy must eventually be worked out by each lay man and woman who responds to the call of Jesus Christ to follow him into this new age. Those who hear Christ's voice must respond with or without the support of their clergy, friends, congregation, or denomination. Those who have the courage, the discipline, and the commitment to respond when Jesus speaks will pull his church forward into the high-tech age.

BACK TO THE MOUNTAIN

This concept of the role of the laity in a church for the high-tech age represents, of course, a single vote. But what if the vote is wrong? What if all of this is merely fireside speculation? What if there is no high-tech age or collision between the Second Wave and the Third Wave? What if you, my fellow laypeople, have no intention of exerting yourselves to develop your hearts or to set out on a personal quest for your own strategy for ministry in a strange and changing world? What if the church as we know it at this moment is all that God has in mind for his people in the twenty-first century? What if each person who reads part 1 is truly satisfied with the role he currently plays and has no interest whatsoever in exploring further? What if closing the book and closing our minds to the future does not really matter? What if there is no call to a personal encounter with the mountain? What if there is no mountain?

If we had been able to actually discuss the issues of part 1 around a fireplace at Paradise Lodge, we could talk until the fire burned down. Step silently now with me out into the darkness of the Rainier night. The evening has a chill.

The sun disappeared into the Pacific hours ago, and we are a mile above sea level as evening settles. The wind speaks as it scurries over the bare rocks and snowfields. A glacier breaks with a thunderous rumble as it crashes over an icefall high above us. The clouds part for just a moment and the moon illuminates the crest of the snowy summit with a pale glow. The mountain is real.

It helps sometimes to think of God as a mountain.

Part Two

A NEW HEART FOR A NEW AGE

3. The Road to a Mature HEART

What is the single most important task we as ordinary Christians can undertake to prepare for life and ministry in the high-tech age? Theologians could debate this question for days and come up with as many answers as there are theologians. But I would like to nominate the task of developing the heart.

My logic is simple. Christians who develop their hearts will make demonstrable progress at getting their act together. And Christians who are getting their act together will be witnesses and ministers to people of the high-tech age whose lives are fragmenting and disintegrating in the midst of the greatest affluence and success in the history of the world.

THE NEED FOR HEART: A PERSONAL STORY

The ideas and concepts I will be presenting in this chapter have come together from an intensely personal struggle on my part to understand my own heart. My investigation of the heart began nearly ten years ago and was not triggered by anything of a religious nature. Instead, it grew out of an article I read in an electrical engineering magazine. In this article, Harvard-trained psychologist Michael Maccoby (the same one mentioned in chapter 1) described his investigation of the work character and the motivation of workers and managers in high-technology industries.

This article sparked my curiosity and I went on to read

Maccoby's book, *The Gamesman*,[1] which reported the final results of that study. Maccoby concluded that all two hundred fifty managers who took part in his seven-year study had highly developed cognitive and intellectual skills. But they were spiritually and emotionally stunted. In particular, they lacked the ability to give and receive love easily, and many lacked the courage of their convictions.

In other words, according to Maccoby and his team of sociopsychologists, these high-tech workers and managers had highly developed heads and underdeveloped hearts. Maccoby concluded *The Gamesman* with a plea for leaders who would develop their hearts as well as their heads.

It took me awhile, but I finally had to admit that, as a high-technology manager, I fit Maccoby's profile personality of a spiritual and emotional pygmy. But at the same time, I knew I was breaking the pattern. Throughout my Christian pilgrimage, Jesus Christ had been working through the power of his Spirit to transform my life.

Because I knew my progress in developing my heart was real, I began to look around me, wondering if I could somehow share with my co-workers in the high-technology community the ideas and disciplines that had helped me.

What I discovered as I looked around was that the problem was more widespread than even Maccoby's book had suggested! Everywhere I looked, I saw evidence of people afflicted with underdeveloped hearts. I had thought that the underdeveloped-heart syndrome was an epidemic that had swept through the high-technology industries and only afflicted high-tech workers. But soon I began to realize that, wherever the high-tech wave spread, the problem was reaching epidemic proportions. Even the church was not spared; this time there was no passover for God's people.

In fact, I have come to believe that the matter of the heart may be the most critical issue facing the church at the onset of the high-tech age! Even though it has had its ups and downs, the church historically has held the keys to life-changing power, power to heal and to develop the heart. (I believe it still does!)

---

1. New York: Simon & Schuster, 1976.

But something happened to the church as the high-tech age rolled in. By the 1970s, for example, North American seminaries were admitting that they had lost touch with the process by which God's power reshapes people's hearts and lives. The seminaries knew very well how to teach theology and the professional skills required to run a church. But across the country—in Catholic and Protestant camps and liberal and conservative strongholds—faculty members were surrendering and admitting that the ability to find God's form for an interior life was an art they had lost.[2]

Even now, as the theological seminaries are trying to recover the ability to give a spiritual form to life, millions of lay men and women are listening to clergy who don't have it and can't teach it! But the laity must have this ability if they are going to move out in effective lay ministries and survive in the world of the high-tech age. How will we get it? I know of no other way than a personal inward strategy for developing the heart. My task in this chapter is to sketch what such a strategy might look like.

A ROAD GUIDE FOR DEVELOPING HEARTS

As a follow-up to *The Gamesman*, Michael Maccoby wrote *The Leader*,[3] which is a collection of case studies of leaders in business and government who serve as positive role models for developed hearts. But at the end, Maccoby was stuck with the dilemma of any secular psychologist who must present a road map for developing the heart. He suggested reading some secular philosophers and even suggested that it might be good to read the Bible. But he was unable to give any practical formula for developing the heart.

After years of study, I have concluded that the single most significant practical resource for development of the heart in the high-tech age is to be found in the Old and New Testament records. But to recommend simply reading

---

2. I gathered these facts from seminars on spiritual formation sponsored in seminaries by Faith at Work. Stan Jones headed the project for Faith at Work, and I served as Seminary Renewal Task Group chairman while on the Faith-at-Work board.

3. New York: Simon & Schuster, 1981.

the Bible leads to a "Catch 22" paradox. To understand the Bible, you need a grasp of the biblical concept of heart. But to grasp the biblical concept of heart, you need to understand the Bible!

I believe that just telling someone to read the Bible in order to learn about the heart is like sending a visitor in Los Angeles out on the freeways without a map or instructions. I still try "free form" navigating in LA myself. The roads are clearly marked, and I cruise on down the freeway until I end up going in circles and becoming thoroughly lost. I may or may not reach my destination, but chances are that I will have a long, hard drive before I finally stop.

What I want to do in this part of the book, therefore, is to provide a simple, practical "road guide" for understanding what the Bible says about developing the heart. I don't claim to be a professional theologian or a biblical scholar. But since I am a Christian with an underdeveloped heart, I have by necessity been on the road toward developing a mature heart for the high-tech age. I hope I can outline a helpful roadmap by drawing on my years of study and experience.

A PROBLEM OF LANGUAGE

I want to begin my description of a practical route to a developed heart by suggesting some ways to get around a major roadblock at the start of the journey. The problem is the English word *heart* used to translate the Hebrew and Greek words. There are three Hebrew words and two Greek words translated into English as *heart,* and they all mean the same thing. But our word *heart* simply isn't adequate to convey that meaning! This is important to realize because, in the Revised Standard Version, *heart* appears nearly a thousand times. If you miss the definition of *heart,* there is at least a possibility of missing the intended meaning of up to a thousand passages. The importance of the concept of the heart surfaces again and again in the next five chapters because I have come to believe the heart is the key to the ministry of the laity.

Understanding the use of the word *heart* in the Bible is a lot like reading road signs in a foreign country with a different language. The first time I decided to drive in Mexico, I had never been there and couldn't read a word of Spanish. I drove my new car across the border at Laredo and pulled into Monterrey on Christmas Eve. It was quitting time and the traffic was going crazy.

It was at this point that I first saw the word *alto* on a road sign. It appeared on what looked to me like a stop sign. I believed it *was* a stop sign—one that like American stop signs means, "Come to a complete stop, look both ways, yield to oncoming traffic, then proceed."

I lived through that first day to tell you that an *alto* sign does not mean "stop"! My enlightened rough translation is: "When you see this sign, speed up, because you're coming to an intersection. And make sure to get up enough speed to have a fighting chance of getting through the intersection first." *Alto* signs are among the most exciting experiences in Mexico—amateur bullfights included!

"Stop" does not adequately translate the Spanish word *alto* on a road sign, any more than the English word *heart* translates the Hebrew-Greek concept of the heart. In order to highlight this difference, from this point on, I will indicate the biblical concept of the heart with capital letters—as "HEART."

What am I saying when I pray with the Psalmist, "Search me, O God, and know my HEART!" (Ps. 139:23)? Where is he going to look? Is God going to go through my pockets, look in my billfold, scrutinize my checkbook? Where is God going to look when he searches me to really know my HEART?

When Jesus designates the top priority commandment, he focuses on the HEART: "You shall love the Lord your God with all your HEART, and with all your soul, and with all your mind, and with all your strength" (Mark 12:30). In order to understand what Christ is getting at, we must grasp the concept behind "with all your HEART."

WHAT HEART IS NOT

On the journey of the HEART through the Scriptures, a number of confusing words pop up on the road signs. It is important to know what the signs do and do not mean. For example, when HEART appears, it very rarely means an organ of the body. The Hebrews knew that there was something that went bumpty bump in their chest, but they knew nothing about its function. They did not know anything about physiology or blood circulation. Like other primitive people, they attributed psychological functions to various organs of the body, but the organs sometimes varied. Some Hebrew passages literally translate, "I love you with all my liver." So the road sign HEART does not mean anatomy or physiology.

The second thing that the HEART is not is the opposite of the head. In *The Gamesman,* Maccoby contrasts the development of the head with the development of the heart. The idea of "opposites" fits our modern understanding, but it conflicts with the biblical concept. When the word *head* appears in the Scriptures, it either means Christ, the head of the church, the organizational top man—or it means the thing that holds your helmet up. When David downed Goliath, he cut off his head to prove that he had won. According to the Bible, the head may be the physical object that sits on top of your body, but it is not the opposite of the HEART.

If the head is not the opposite of HEART, perhaps the *mind* is. The phrase "HEART and mind" does appear in Scripture. And the word *mind* definitely describes mental functions such as meditation, diagnostic thinking, analytical thinking, and various mental manipulations. But the Hebrews were not precise in chopping up word meanings and had no interest in dividing up human life into little categories like we do today. In the English Old Testament, the word that is commonly translated "mind" could more accurately be translated "heart"! In other words, the words *mind* and *heart* as used in the Bible are similar, not opposites.

Several other road signs which are sometimes confused with the HEART appear in this biblical journey. *HEART* and *soul* often appear together but do not mean the same thing. In Scripture, the word *soul* describes the life force in a physical body. If you add a soul and a body together, you get a living being. If the soul starts to fade on you, death is coming.

Biblically speaking, the presence of a soul indicates whether a physical being is dead or alive. If the computer is taken as a modern analogy, the body is the case and frame and the soul is the little red "on" light that indicates the power is on and the circuits are working. The HEART, on the other hand, would refer to that functioning collection of circuits and microchips known as the central processor unit.

Still another road sign sometimes confused with HEART is the one labeled "spirit." The presence of a spirit indicates that something is alive which doesn't have a body. A living physical body has a soul, but God or the devil or anything that is alive but does not have a physical body has a spirit. The Hebrews saw the Holy Spirit as God's life force existing apart from a physical body. The temptation to use *spirit, soul,* and *HEART* interchangeably is dangerous from a biblical standpoint, because each one represents a unique and useful concept quite distinct from the others.

FIVE DIMENSIONS OF THE HEART

The biblical HEART has five unique dimensions that characterize a human life. Like the five facets of a finely cut gemstone, each dimension gives a unique insight into the nature of a human being. (The HEART also reflects the fact that we are actually made in God's image since the HEART of God is regularly mentioned by the biblical writers.)

As a physicist, I work with light. And I like to compare the HEART to "white" light, which actually contains all the colors of the rainbow. When a glass prism is placed in the path of a beam of white light, the red, orange, yellow, green, blue, and violet components are spread out so they can be seen and studied separately. In the same way, we can better understand the HEART as it appears in Scripture if we "spread out" its individual dimensions.

The first dimension is the *emotional dimension.* Here, the Hebrew most nearly matches the English usage in picturing the HEART as the seat of the emotions. But the biblical writers always allow the HEART to cover an emotional range of positive as well as negative extremes. English usage

61

often sentimentalizes by attributing only good emotions to the heart. In the Scriptures, the HEART is fully capable of negative, as well as positive, emotions. The HEART will produce love, but it will also be the source of hate. The emotional dimension of the HEART described by biblical writers covers the total range of human emotions.

The *volitional dimension* of the HEART refers to the will. And this dimension also ranges from positive to negative extremes. From the HEART may come the will to do what is called a courageous act. From the HEART can also come another kind of action that is cowardly betrayal. In its volitional dimension, the HEART runs the total spectrum of the human will.

The *ethical dimension* introduces the reality of good and evil. Ethics ultimately deal with the knowledge of these two polarities. The HEART has the ability to soak up either good or evil like a sponge. But the HEART is also like a computer. It will accumulate good or evil according to what is loaded into it. Discernment of good and evil in our lives and world is the function of the ethical dimension of the heart.

The *intellectual dimension* seems strangely out of place to us in English-speaking countries. We are so used to dealing with the "head and the heart" as opposites that we almost require a cultural reprogramming to grasp the biblical idea that the human intellect resides in the HEART. The biblical goal for the intellect is the understanding of God's ways. According to the Bible, if I truly give my HEART to Jesus, I give my intellect to him as part of the deal.

The *spiritual dimension* is the final dimension of the HEART—and even secular psychologists recognize that a great many people in the high-tech age lead spiritually stunted lives. The search for a solution to this problem must eventually come face-to-face with the issue of spiritual values versus spiritual reality. What does God actually do when we pray? Is there reality to the claim that the Christ is God alive in our midst? Was J. B. Phillips correct when he said that God has visited an alien planet? From the biblical standpoint, the HEART deals not only with spiritual values, but also with the reality of Christ, who is alive and at work through his spirit in the world today. The spiritual dimension of the HEART is the point of contact with God.

I believe that the church for the high-tech age must gamble its future on lay men and women who have an internal strategy—ordinary Christians who have opened up their intellects, emotions, ethics, and wills to God at a point of authentic contact with spiritual reality. As God reveals his thoughts, feelings, discernment of good and evil, and will, people's HEARTs grow and are transformed. The goal of an interior strategy of the HEART is to reshape the interior of our lives according to God's plans for the HEART. When this happens, God can use his people to reshape the church and the world.

4. The Volitional Dimension

My first serious encounter with the Christian faith came at the point of the volitional dimension of the HEART. I was confronted by a fascinating image of God which has refused to fade or dim, even in this high-tech age. My life took a definite turn at that moment, even though I knew nothing about the will or the HEART with all its dimensions.

At the time, I was a high-school student and had made my spiritual home in the Presbyterian church of a small Oklahoma town. I played a lot of Ping-Pong, was active in the youth group, and even held a presbytery office. I was not all that sure who this Jesus Christ was supposed to be, but the Christian life was something I thought I wanted in on.

AN ENCOUNTER WITH CHRIST

The summer before I left home to begin a high-tech career at the university, I spent a week among the ghosts of America's frontier. I attended a student conference on the campus of a former Indian mission school. Like the young Cherokees who had studied at the school, I discovered, for the first time, a Bible in my native tongue—modern English (the first edition of the Revised Standard Version). Each morning after breakfast, I would find a rock or tree where I could sit alone in silence for prayer and meditation.

As I read the "quiet time" booklet one morning, the following words reached into my mind and totally captured my imagination: "The demands of Christ are hard, unutterably

64

hard, for those who resist. But for those who submit, the yoke is easy and the burden is light." (Years later, I discovered that these lines were written by the German theologian and pastor Dietrich Bonhoeffer in a book called *The Cost of Discipleship*.[1])

The message was quite clear. I saw that I was not dealing with some remote, abstract, shadowy grandfather figure of a God out there somewhere. I sensed that, in Jesus Christ, God was very near. I saw that this Christ was personally interested in my life, in what I did day by day, and that true peace, meaning, and purpose for my life would come through following this Christ.

I had no idea what this meant in practical terms or how to respond. All I could do was to place the page from the booklet in my Bible and set out in hope of discovering the Christ and the life described in Bonhoeffer's words.

This life and this Christ became a reality for me during the following year through an unusual consortium of Christians on the University of Oklahoma campus. Two of my fraternity brothers lured me with hot popcorn out of my usual rounds of study, dating, football, and rock-'n'-roll to meet with them for Bible study each Thursday night. On Friday nights, we would visit a home near the campus to listen to people talk about their encounters with Jesus Christ.

The Friday-night meetings were hosted by a team from a new and sometimes suspect organization called Campus Crusade for Christ. Those who spoke were laypeople and clergy, students and professors, husbands and wives, business people and professionals. This parade of witnesses included people from Young Life, Navigators, Billy Graham teams—and even the senior minister of my own Presbyterian church in Oklahoma City. I was hit hardest by the witness of young businessmen like Bill Yinger from my church and Keith Miller, who had been president of my social fraternity a few years earlier.

I listened to the many variations on the same theme: "What Life Was Like Apart from Jesus Christ" versus "What

---

1. New York: Macmillan, 1949.

Life Is Like with Jesus Christ." Each week in the fraternity Bible study, the three of us would read the Gospel of John and try to figure out what claims Jesus actually made about himself. For several years, I listened and studied. At the same time, I continued to progress in my engineering, science, and mathematics classes.

I gradually found myself convinced that Jesus Christ is the force behind the physical universe, the author of the mysteries that I planned to probe as a career. The question was not whether God was real. The question was whether God thought *I* was real. The historic witness of my church, the witness of the biblical record, and the Friday night panorama of local witnesses all converged on the same answer: God loves me and cares about sharing his life with me through Jesus Christ.

TIME TO CHOOSE

Finally, I was face-to-face with the issue of the will, the volitional dimension of the HEART. What would I personally choose to do with Jesus Christ? Over the months, I had collected all the facts and evidence I needed. When I finally looked inward and saw the self-centeredness and selfishness that were at the core of my being, I knew what I must do. I sat in my room one afternoon and prayed, "Christ, if you are real and really come into people's lives, I want you to come into mine. Come into my heart and run my life. I commit this mess to you if you will take care of it!" This simple invitation was the act of the will that began my personal relationship with Jesus Christ.

My decision to accept Jesus Christ was the culmination of a long process, although for some people it appears to happen instantly. The critical issue is establishing a personal relationship with God as he is made known through Jesus Christ. Knowledge of salvation comes in that instant, although full conversion of the HEART can take a lifetime.

When Jesus Christ responds to my invitation to come into my life and HEART, the drama of the volitional dimension of the HEART unfolds in a new act. There are now two wills to consider: God's will and my will. As in any relationship involving two people, these two wills can be in agreement or in opposition. As I see it, an important goal of our interior strategy must be to work through conflict and uncertainty to reach a HEART-to-HEART agreement with God and act on it.

Issues of the volitional dimension of the HEART fall into a number of standard categories. I will look at three in order to sketch the process of developing this dimension.

A MATTER OF TREASURE

A major issue of the will has always been *the setting of life's priorities.* Because of the incredibly high standard of living and widespread affluence in the high-tech age, this is even more critical today. Competition for each day's "prime time" is fierce.

Jesus made the setting of priorities a matter of the HEART when he said, "Fear not, little flock, for it is your Father's good pleasure to give you the kingdom. Sell your possessions, and give alms; provide yourselves with purses that do not grow old, with a treasure in the heavens that does not fail, where no thief approaches and no moth destroys. For where your treasure is, there will your HEART be also" (Luke 12:32–34).

The important concept in this passage, as far as the high-tech age is concerned, is the concept of a "treasure." A treasure is something that is of great value and highly prized. It is also something that is *accumulated.* It is something we acquire and must hold onto, protect, and preserve.

In this passage, Jesus was saying that spiritual valuables—not the valuables of the world—should be our treasures. Wealth, power, and material goods, as well as intellectual and artistic abilities, can either be items of stewardship, passing through our lives for our benefit and the benefit of others, or they can be the treasures that we lock onto. Jesus probes the HEART to discover the "white knuckle" treasures we hold on to too tightly.

Our interior strategy must expect and allow space for

regular "treasure inventories." When the things of the world become treasures, rather than matters of stewardship that are open to God's direction in their use and disposal, the HEART is paralyzed in its growth and development.

According to this Scripture passage, Christ holds us accountable for setting our priorities and selecting our treasures. And the reason stated by Jesus is that the treasure pulls the HEART to it.

My wife is a student of art history. And since I began work on this book, I have followed her to view several major collections of paintings. Last year, as I viewed the first major exhibit of Dégas paintings, I saw what an enormous job it was to display, preserve, and protect a major art treasure. This helped me to see what Jesus meant when he said that where your treasure is, your heart will also be. The treasure will consume the HEART of the one who possesses it.

Each dimension of the HEART is drawn into this issue of treasure. My intellectual energy will focus on the treasure. My understanding of right and wrong, good and evil, can be distorted to benefit the treasure. I will become deeply involved emotionally with the treasure. If I put the treasure first in my life and it brings me into direct conflict with God's will, my contact with God will dim and fade.

Treasures will come and go in my life, but the task of the interior strategy is to open up the HEART and abandon to God those treasures that do not qualify as "treasures in heaven."

As I have worked to start a new business these last few years, I have had some dark, dry periods. I have found myself commuting long distances for months at a time, trying to complete projects that seemed to have no end. I am embarrassed and amazed at how angry and irritated I have gotten with God when I momentarily tried to blame him for the obstacles in my path.

Looking back, I realize that God needed to bring me to the edge of disaster to show me that whatever project I was working on could become a personal treasure instead of a challenging assignment to build a company as a servant of God and of my customers.

THE VOLITIONAL DIMENSION

At a time when I was facing the possibility that I could go no farther with my business, I was given the autobiography of a man named Fredrik (Frits) Philips.[2] During World War II, Frits was running his father's company in Holland under German occupation. With thirty-five thousand employees, this firm was the largest in Holland and certainly qualified as a prized high-tech treasure.

Each day as the war continued, new rumors came that the company was about to be taken over by German companies. Frits feared that the great company built by his uncle and his father would disappear into Nazi Germany. But one day, as he sought God's guidance, he sensed God pointing out to him that there was nothing he could do to determine if the company was ultimately to succeed or fail, stay or disappear. God's word for Frits was simply to do his best that day.

If the company was Frits Philips's treasure, it would have been appropriate for him to go to the frenzied limit—to fight and maneuver with the Nazis to hold the company. But if Christ was the treasure of his life, he could take God's guidance seriously, relax, and set out to be God's person at work, doing his best each day. This is what he chose to do. He demonstrated a personal interior strategy that allowed his will to converge with God's will. And the result was an inner freedom in his high-tech world—an attitude that caused great frustration for his Nazi overseers.

LOSING HEART

Christ's teaching on treasure speaks directly to the conflict between our will and God's will over priorities of life. A second issue of the will that occurs frequently in the Scriptures is the *loss of will*. When conditions appear so terrible that there seems to be no point in going on, we can lose HEART. The conflict between our will and God's will, in this case, is over giving up or hanging in there.

Loss of HEART can come from either depression or despair. When I am gripped by depression, there seems to

---

2. Fredrik Philips, *45 Years with Philips* (Poole: Blandford Press, 1978).

be no point in going forward. I feel that the situation is hopeless no matter what the true facts are. Despair is an appropriate response to situations that can be objectively declared to be without hope. The apostle Paul described a time, during a storm at sea on his journey from Jerusalem to Rome, when despair really was an appropriate response to the situation: "And when neither sun nor stars appeared for many a day, and no small tempest lay on us, all hope of our being saved was at last abandoned" (Acts 27:20).

But even in times when despair is appropriate, there is hope. Jesus can read the human HEART and can energize and revitalize the will of a "lost HEART" with the single phrase, "Take HEART."

When a paralytic was brought to him for healing, Jesus said: "Take HEART, your sins are forgiven." A nameless woman, who had hemorrhaged internally for twelve years, slipped through the crowd to touch his garment. When Jesus singled her out, he said, "Take HEART. Your faith has made you whole." His own disciples became terrified when they saw Jesus walking on the water, because they literally thought they had seen a ghost. Jesus again said, "Take HEART. It is I. Have no fear."

In each case, people came close to Christ and were so shocked and surprised by the encounter that Jesus had to steady and encourage them by saying, "Take HEART." Out in the high-tech world when the going gets tough, I need to hear Christ's voice saying to me personally, "Take HEART." When Christ makes his power and presence felt in the day-to-day world where I live and work, I welcome his voice saying to me, "Take HEART."

DEVELOPING THE VOLITIONAL DIMENSION

A third issue of the will that crops up frequently in Scripture is development of the volitional dimension of the HEART. God desires to be involved in my life in far greater depth than merely sending down answers to the "big" questions of whom I should marry, where I should live, and what job I should take. These questions are indeed

70

important! But the great majority of the issues of the will must be worked out each day as I discover guidance in God's written word and apply it to my life. A new freedom comes as I open up the volitional dimension of my HEART to God daily and try to get my will synchronized with his will.

When ordinary Christians follow Jesus Christ into the high-tech world that is our natural habitat, the going can often be tough and lonely and the territory uncharted. There are no guarantees of prosperity and success in the world's arena. As Bonhoeffer said in that quote which first confronted me with the fact that Christ makes demands of anyone who follows him, discipleship can be costly.

Bonhoeffer's words were based on Jesus' discussion of a goal for development of the volitional dimension of the HEART: Jesus said, "I thank thee, Father, Lord of heaven and earth, that thou hast hidden these things from the wise and understanding and revealed them to babes." It is clear from this statement that the interior strategy for the HEART must be practical, understandable, and workable.

But then Jesus continued, "Yea, Father, for such was thy gracious will. All things have been delivered to me by my Father; and no one knows the Son except the Father, and no one knows the Father except the Son and any one to whom the Son chooses to reveal him. Come to me, all who labor and are heavy laden, and I will give you rest. Take my yoke upon you, and learn from me; for I am gentle and lowly in HEART, and you will find rest for your souls. For my yoke is easy, and my burden is light" (Matt. 11:25–30).

This passage underscores the fact that the truth is simple, and it must be as simple in the high-tech age as it was in the age of the Roman Empire. Those who know Christ know God. There may be a streak of humor in Jesus' offer to turn his own burden over to people who are already so loaded down that they are worn out. Yet, Jesus' offer to exchange burdens is a serious offer. And when I turn my load over to Christ and pick up his burden, the result is a peace and freedom that arise out of finding ultimate meaning and purpose to my life.

This exchange is the goal for developing the volitional

71

dimension of the HEART. I will to do God's will—not for an instant, but for the long haul. When Jesus urges me to be "lowly in HEART" like him, I interpret this to mean that Jesus was not too great to do the will of the Father. His intellect was not so powerful that he could not invest it in serving the Father. His emotions were not so strong, his spiritual charisma so great, or his insight into issues of good and evil so keen that he could ignore his Father's will.

As Jesus served the Father, he invites his followers to take up the same yoke for the same task. When Jesus performed acts of service for the Father here on earth, he did it by the power of the Holy Spirit. He made his body available and God made the power available.

Today, in the high-tech age, *we* are the Lord's body. The power of the Holy Spirit is still available to work in and through the body of Christ, the church. Jesus put the goal for the volitional dimension of the HEART on a very personal and practical level. Do I will to do God's will day by day, moment by moment?

An effective interior strategy for developing the HEART must chip away at the task of abandoning my will to God, so that I can be about the business of doing God's will with the same power that was available to Jesus—the power of the Holy Spirit, which is present today within my HEART.

HOW TO MAKE THE YOKE LIGHT

Thirty years ago, I first read Bonhoeffer's words: "The demands of Christ are hard, unutterably hard, for those who resist. But for those who submit the yoke is easy and the burden is light!" I gambled my life on the hope that three things are true: that God is near and not far off; that in Christ, God loves and cares for me personally; and that peace, meaning, and purpose will come as I discover God's will and do it.

All three have proven to be true. I have found in these truths the ground rules for being God's person in the high-tech age.

But I still struggle with the demands of Christ. I believe that Christ is calling me to follow him out into the high-tech world to minister and serve. I believe that Christ is calling the laity of his church to this task. If I resist these demands (perhaps because my church is not quite ready), Christ's yoke will be unbearably heavy.

What is it that makes the yoke so heavy? What does "resisting" mean? When I look at the exterior areas of my life where I must seek God's will about what job to take, whom to marry, or which church to join, I get a vivid picture of a "crisis at the crossroads." And I begin to argue with myself that "resisting" means taking the wrong fork in the road, missing God's guidance either because of ignorance or defiance. But these crucial moments don't come around often, and I believe there is more to the heavy yoke than that.

When the will is seen as a dimension of the HEART, it becomes a part of my interior life. God has laid out in his word guidelines to which I must submit every moment of every waking day, not just at life's crossroads.

Perhaps a more accurate picture is that of a family table! I am a member of God's family. Christ and my Christian brothers and sisters know my HEART, my skills and aptitudes, the unique gifts that the Holy Spirit has placed in my life to serve the family. Christ himself knows the purpose of my life, what God had in mind when he created me, even if it has never been fully shown to me.

The heavy yoke presses down when I push away from the table and turn my back on the family. The demands of Christ become unbearably hard when I ignore the family lifestyle and set out on my own venture alone. But the burden becomes light when I invest my life and all my gifts and resources in God's family business.

I have noticed that my "crises of the crossroads" situations have a way of working themselves out smoothly when I have developed the volitional dimension of my HEART by working each day in God's family business. So I turn again and again to a simple three-sentence prayer of the HEART that brings me back to this task of seeking God's will each day: "Lord, I commit my life afresh to you this day. I commit this day to you. Keep me in the stream of your Spirit this day. In Jesus' name."

5. The Emotional Dimension

The emotional dimension of the HEART comes closest to the meaning of the English word *heart*. Of the five dimensions of the HEART, this may be the one least developed in the high-tech age.

As I said in an earlier chapter, psychologist Michael Maccoby used the term "underdeveloped heart" to describe high-technology managers who were emotionally (as well as spiritually) stunted. And this emotionally stunted state is the starting point from which many of us must start in devising an interior strategy for emotional development of the HEART.

But why go to all the trouble and pain of working toward emotional maturity? After all, emotional underdevelopment is an acceptable standard for the high-tech age. As long as I am creative, innovative, and highly productive in my work, I can get away with being an emotional pygmy. If my marriage fails and my family disintegrates, I can still go to work, do my job, and fit into the high-tech culture with its epidemic of broken relationships.

And it's not just a matter of our high-tech culture *accepting* emotional underdevelopment. The rapid pace and high stress level of our society can push us toward and even *reward* us for ignoring the emotional dimension of the HEART. Pressures at work and home, instant media links to events of violence and famine anywhere in the world, the blinding speed at which we live—all these can make it seem easier sometimes just to "shut down" emotionally in order to protect ourselves.

THE EMOTIONAL DIMENSION

THE CALL TO EMOTIONAL MATURITY

Who issues the call, then for an audit of the emotional dimension in our lives? What can motivate people of the high-tech age to move toward emotional maturity?

In my own life, it has been the voice of Christ calling me to grow emotionally as well as in the other dimensions of my life. And he has often had to shout for me to hear! Just keeping in touch with my feelings and emotions has always been tough for me—much less dealing with them in a mature manner.

My continuing struggle with the emotional dimension of my life came to a head several years ago, when I was trying to start a new business. In the entrepreneurial excitement of a new venture, visions of high-tech sugarplums were dancing in my head. But I was also under a lot of emotional stress. The brutal reality is that nine out of ten new companies fail in the first five years. Those who try this path walk an emotional tightrope over a yawning chasm of disaster, not knowing if they will be heros or failures.

After eighteen months with the new company, I had an unusual opportunity to take an audit of my own emotional condition and maturity. It was a crisis time in the company; both my chief engineer and head consultant had given up on our first new product-development project and walked away. We had spent twice as much on the project as had originally been budgeted, and we still did not know if it was technically possible to build the product and make money on it.

At this point, I took a break to attend a contemplative retreat at Laity Lodge. I spent a week on this beautiful Texas hill-country ranch, alone with God in silence and study.

This experience of suddenly crashing into silence and stillness was an emotional culture shock! At the start of the week, I was aware of the fact that I had stress in my life. In fact, every day in the previous year, I had prayed for the courage and endurance to keep going. But now, in the quiet of the river bank, I was almost overwhelmed with a horde of feelings I didn't even know were there—feelings

I kept shoved below the surface of my life. I realized that in the past months I had fallen into my oldest pattern of dealing with stress: "Don't talk! Don't feel! Just keep your head down and charge ahead!" And by responding in this way to the stress of my job, I had begun to isolate myself from family, friends, God—all those who could help me handle the stress I was under.

During the times of worship, study, and silence that made up that week at Laity Lodge, I faced my pervasive fears about making a living. I did not know if I was going broke or on my way to success, and in the meantime I needed to support my family—which was tough on intermittent cash flow and missed paychecks. I was afraid of failure and the prospect of either going back to my old job or finding a new one. And I felt guilt over forcing my family to sacrifice both money and quality time together for my dream project. The fear of having made a mistake in reading God's guidance to take this radical, high-risk vocational path also nagged at me.

What was happening to me at that retreat was that I was gradually allowing God the freedom to penetrate the emotional sphere of my life in order to bring growth and balance. This is the challenge of the emotional dimension of the HEART. And it is not just a one-time thing. Part of the interior strategy of the HEART must be opening the emotional dimension to God on a daily basis. This may be easy for some, but it has never been easy for me. I have to remind myself that it is always worthwhile, even if it is sometimes painful.

One morning while still at Laity Lodge, I took the Scripture assigned for meditation and made my way down the canyon wall to a special place, a ledge overhanging a deep pool in the Frio River. I leaned back against a rock wall to focus on the words of Jesus: "Therefore I tell you, do not be anxious about your life, what you shall eat or what you shall drink, nor about your body, what you shall put on. Is not life more than food, and the body more than clothing? Look at the birds of the air: they neither sow nor reap nor gather into barns, and yet your heavenly Father feeds them. . . .

And which of you by being anxious can add one cubit to his span of life?" (Matt. 6:25–27).

As I read these verses, I was drawn to the phrase, "Do not be anxious about your life." As I repeated this verse over and over, God seemed to say that I could be free of the swirl of anxieties, the pool of diffuse fears that I had been holding submerged below the conscious level in my HEART.

I let the words, "do not be anxious," ring in my head as I worked my way out onto the ledge and—holding firmly to a cedar limb—leaned out to look up and down the river. Suddenly, two objects headed straight toward me from the opposite bank. I dodged with the same reflex used to avoid something headed straight into a car windshield. The objects veered into the next cedar—two brilliant Mexican cardinals in spectacular hues of red and brown. They preened for several minutes a few meters away, and God seemed to speak: "Look at the birds of the air."

God had broken into my high-tech venture and forced me to acknowledge that I must trust him with my whole life—including my emotions.

THE BIBLICAL VIEW OF EMOTIONS

Modern psychology has given us some marvelous insights into the emotional sphere of our lives and the relationship between emotions and behavior. But sometimes, in looking into the roots of why we feel the way we do, psychology has overlooked the issue of responsibility. The biblical concept of HEART places the responsibility for behavior that arises from feelings squarely on the individual without regard for heredity, environment, or social norms.

The biblical concept of the HEART continually presents emotions and feelings as natural, but neutral—in themselves neither good nor bad. God holds us accountable not for the emotions we experience (which we can't avoid), but rather for how we deal with them.

The issue of the emotional dimension of the HEART is complicated by the fact that the English usage of *heart* lacks the comprehensive emotional scope of the biblical HEART.

The emotional dimension of the heart in popular English points to sincere, positive, and admirable emotions with a touch of heroic or laughable sentimentality. If I say I write from the heart, I mean that my true feelings and emotions motivated me. If a writer visits ninety-nine publishers before his book is finally published, we say that he has real heart—the courage to keep going in the face of overwhelming opposition. If I blow my first royalty check on a present for my wife, you will say my heart got the best of me. (My wife says it will never happen!)

The biblical HEART neatly sidesteps this kind of usage, however, and presents the HEART as the source of a *full spectrum* of human emotions. These emotions range from love to hostility and hate and have tremendous power for good and for evil.

FORGIVENESS—A KEY TO EMOTIONAL MATURITY

The goal for the emotional dimension of the HEART is emotional maturity, which must always be defined with the help of the spiritual, ethical, intellectual, and volitional dimensions. The biblical writers and the teachings of Jesus continually point to constructive rather than destructive ways to deal with the emotions of the HEART.

An example of this contructive emphasis is the concept of forgiveness. Learning to accept God's forgiveness and to forgive others and myself is an important step toward achieving maturity in the emotional dimension of the heart.

I have always had difficulty dealing with anger and aggressive feelings, particularly when I feel I have been wronged or my rights violated. Something inside me has always said, "Don't get mad; just get even"—and the trouble is, I have tended to get mad as well as even! (In fact, I avoid putting Christian bumper stickers on my car because I don't want to give God a bad name with my driving.)

That is why I relate so well to Simon Peter, who asked Jesus, "Lord, how often shall my brother sin against me, and I forgive him? As many as seven times?" I am sure that number seemed as generously large to Peter as it does to me. But Jesus replied, "I do not say to you seven times, but seventy times seven" (Matt. 18:21–22). Incredible! If Jesus was serious, he must have a new and innovative way to deal with the emotional dimension of the HEART.

I believe not only that Jesus was serious, but that he intended this boundless forgiveness as an ordinary lifestyle for those who have given their HEARTs to him. Jesus followed his seventy-times-seven comment to Peter in the eighteenth chapter of Matthew with a story that introduces the concept of forgiveness as an essential ingredient of the kingdom of heaven—and a crucial element in emotional maturity.

Jesus described the kingdom of heaven by using a down-to-earth story about two men who had been lending money and decided to call in their loans. The first man was a king who decided to settle the outstanding debts of his servants. One servant turned up with an account overdue to the tune of fifteen years of his wages—more than he could ever repay.

When the king learned the debt could not be paid, he ordered the servant and his family sold as slaves. But the servant fell on his knees and made an emotional, moving plea for the opportunity to repay his debt in full. The king responded by forgiving the debt and setting him free. (At this point, Jesus introduced the reality of guilt by referring to this man's enormous unpaid debt. He also introduced the two options for dealing with such a huge amount of guilt: forgiveness or punishment.)

After being released, the servant who had been forgiven ran into a co-worker who owed him a day's wages. The man grabbed his co-worker by the throat and demanded payment. He ignored the man's plea for more time to pay and had him thrown in jail until he could pay in full. When the king got word of this injustice, he was so enraged that he ordered the man he had forgiven to be tortured until he paid in full. (By describing this minor debt, which had little financial significance but which nevertheless aroused a real emotional response and a punishment far more extreme than the debt warranted, Jesus introduced the idea

79

that our responses to guilt can be out of proportion to the reality of our actual guilt. This relates directly to the issue of real guilt, which can either be forgiven or punished, and false guilt, which must be dismissed and abandoned to God.)

Jesus concludes the story with this line: "So also my heavenly Father will do to every one of you, if you do not forgive your brother from your HEART" (Matt. 18:23–35).

This R-rated tale ("R" for violence) sets forgiveness in a swirl of powerful emotions. As Christ's followers, we are left with the astounding realization that, like the first servant, our debt before God in terms of accumulated, continuing sin is so great that God must either punish us or forgive us—there is simply no way that we could work it off in fifteen years or fifteen million years. And the amazing thing is that God chooses to forgive us! But he expects us to develop the emotional maturity to forgive both ourselves and others.

Incidentally, the key ingredient of forgiveness, strange as it may sound, is guilt. Without guilt there is nothing to forgive. As I listen to the story about the king and the two debtors, I identify with the king's servant who reacts violently to the guilt of others while he is a thousand times more guilty. Guilt tends to be an emotionally loaded subject; it can drop like a boulder into a calm, quiet mountain pool of well-contained emotions, causing a huge splash and sending waves in all directions. In an instant, the emotional dimension of the HEART is laid bare.

But if forgiveness is one of the keys to developing the emotional dimension of the HEART, how do we learn to forgive both others or ourselves? The emotions of anger and resentment and guilt are real. Are we supposed to just bury them—simply "forgive and forget"? Anyone who has ever tried knows it's not that easy!

HOW CAN WE FORGIVE?

An important first step toward practicing forgiveness of the HEART is deciding whether the guilt is real guilt or false guilt. It is possible to blame others or ourselves for events and actions for which the person receiving the blame cannot be held responsible. The guilt *feelings* are real, but there is no real guilt.

Swiss physician Dr. Paul Tournier says in his book, *Guilt and Grace*[1] that his waiting room was filled with people afflicted with false guilt—eaten away by guilty feelings about events over which they had no control. In the story Jesus told, real guilt rested with the servant who had run up a debt more than fifteen times his annual salary and could not pay. By contrast, the servant who borrowed one day's salary from his fellow worker to get to payday was indeed liable for his debt, but he was not guilty of the gross financial mismanagement the first servant accused him of. The first servant's anger toward him and threatened punishment was inappropriate because he was assigning false guilt. Because it *is* false, this kind of guilt cannot be forgiven or punished; the only way of handling it is to correctly identify it and abandon to God the inappropriate feelings of guilt or anger.

Once any kind of guilt has been identified, the temptation is to trot out the old bromide: "forgive and forget." But I believe such a simplistic solution short-circuits the powerful process of forgiveness of the HEART. Besides, we cannot magically "forget" feelings away. Guilt may be real or false, but the feelings are always real. When someone wrongs me, rejects me, or takes something that is mine, I become angry and hostile. When I fail to measure up to my own standards or meet personal goals, I feel angry at myself and guilty.

The next step toward forgiveness, then, is not to "forget" these feelings, but to "own" them—to recognize them, name them, acknowledge their reality and power. Remember, the feelings are just as real for false guilt as for real guilt.

Self-destructive behavior on the part of many of the "flower children" of the 1960s has been traced to false guilt over their privileged upbringing. In a similar vein, I

---

1. New York: Harper, 1958.

remember reading about a down-and-out young woman whose psychiatrist traced the downward spiral of her life to guilt over *just being alive.* Her strict Christian parents had passed to their daughter the shame and guilt they felt over the pregnancy that had forced them to marry. And the daughter, who was not at fault, was being destroyed by inappropriate feelings of guilt.

As I have already indicated, if the guilt is false, we need to hand our feelings over to God—to give them up because they are inappropriate. If the guilt is real, the next step is to deal with it. And whether we are talking about our own guilt or the guilt of others, there are only two options for dealing with it: forgiveness or punishment. And the Bible makes it clear that our Lord has chosen the path of forgiveness.

Once again, I do not believe that forgiveness means forgetting. The New Testament says nothing about forgetting either the event that caused the guilt or the feelings associated with it. What forgiveness really means is *deliberately giving up on punishment.* Whether I hold someone else or even myself guilty, I choose not to punish the guilty party.

This kind of forgiveness has no room for "yes, buts." It must be complete in each dimension of the HEART. This means there can be no emotional punishment. (Some families have specialized in punishing guilty family members by cutting them off from any emotional contact with the rest of the family.) There can be no intellectual punishment—no satisfying schemes and plots for "sweet mental revenge." The will is bound and prohibited from taking action to punish, even when the opportunity to get even comes. Ethical punishment—choosing evil over good for the guilty person—is not an option. Perhaps the most difficult to give up is spiritual punishment—saying, "I give up but I hope God will get them."

Please understand that when I say "punishment" I am not talking about *discipline.* Nowhere does Jesus attempt to do away with the need for discipline and order in a society of people who must live together as families and communities. There is an important difference between discipline—

82

which is done for the purpose of teaching and training and keeping order—and punishment.

What I believe Jesus was saying in the story about the two debtors is that forgiveness is one of the key principles on which the kingdom of heaven operates! No follower of Jesus can forget that God's forgiveness is what brings each person into God's presence. The family of God is a family of grace, not of guiltlessness. And when we recognize that and let it penetrate the emotional dimension of our lives, we take a big step toward emotional maturity.

What does all this mean to the ordinary Christian in the high-tech world? Either Jesus was a visionary dreamer, or forgiveness of the HEART is a concept that can compete on its own merits in the arenas of life today. Forgiveness is a system of living that allows me to abandon to God my need to punish—with its costly use of time and emotional energy. I can bring false guilt to God to be freed of it. The feelings that churn in my HEART can be laid before God for healing. Through the experience of God's forgiveness, I can learn to forgive myself and others.

LOVE IN THE EMOTIONAL DIMENSION

Forgiveness—release from a need to punish—is a single example of the freedom that comes with maturity in the emotional dimension of the HEART. This freedom allows us to reach for the goal of emotional development pointed to by Jesus when he described the Great Commandments: "The first is, 'Hear, O Israel: The Lord our God, the Lord is one; and you shall love the Lord your God with all your HEART, and with all your soul, and with all your mind, and with all your strength.' The second is this, 'You shall love your neighbor as yourself' " (Mark 12:29–32).

In that moment, Jesus dimmed every other issue and illuminated the human HEART as a source of *love* that points like a beam of light straight to the Lord God. The beam swings slowly around to other people, then finally reflects back into our own lives. As I listen to the words of Jesus, the intensity of this love in my own life grows and swells, and I am freed in Christ to put my total mental and physical strength, my total life force, and the resources of all five dimensions of my HEART into the love that goes out from me.

This love for the Lord and for the significant people in my life—myself included—requires the total resources of the HEART. It certainly includes removing roadblocks of emotional immaturity. But it also involves expressing love with my intellect, with my choices in issues of good and evil, with my will to action for the ones I love. I must tap my spiritual resources and let the love of God pour through my life.

THE HIGH-TECH WAR AGAINST EMOTIONAL MATURITY

I said at the beginning of this chapter that the emotional dimension of the HEART is probably the least developed in the high-tech age, and that in our high-tech culture many of us are in danger of becoming emotional pygmies.

Part of the reason for this is that attempts to develop the emotional dimension of the HEART are quickly met with opposition from the prevailing culture. Attacks come from many fronts, and an effective interior strategy for developing the HEART in the high-tech age must be prepared to counter them.

One standard tactic of attack is simply to divert the HEART to success and achievement in the intellectual arenas. The idea is that no one will audit my HEART if I am a winner, a success.

A second tactic designed to divert the HEART from the quest for emotional maturity is to destroy the energy balance in a person's life. If I am totally exhausted from trivial pursuits offered by the high-tech age, I have no energy left to practice the kind of forgiveness Jesus speaks about. If my emotional battery is dead from driving, flying, playing, working, and buying, I have no emotional spark left for the costly love of God, my neighbor, or myself.

A third attack on the emotional dimension of the HEART

comes from the inside. Emotional development is blocked by inertia, the tendency we all have to want to stay in the state we are in without serious thoughtful growth or change.

Our society is full of people who are leading mildly to severely damaged emotional lives. The emotional dimension of their HEARTs may have been battered by traumatic situations such as alcohol or drug dependency, growing up in a family with an addictive parent, physical or sexual abuse, or divorce. It may have been dulled and blunted by overemphasis on the material things of life or strangled by self-protectiveness in a stressful world. There is always the temptation in any of these situations simply to give up and stay put emotionally—the cost of growth seems too much.

The call of Christ, however, is "Come to me and be made whole." An interior strategy for developing the HEART must lay out a practical route leading toward emotional wholeness and maturity. In some cases, this may involve obtaining professional psychological or psychiatric help. And it always involves enlisting *the help of other people.*

In my own experience, participation in small groups dedicated to spiritual and emotional growth has been the single most valuable resource for stimulating growth in the emotional dimension of my life. One type of group first meets to take a standard psychological test, which is "graded" by a Christian psychologist. The test results profile each group member's personality. Then the group members use the personality profiles as tools for praying about, meditating on, and studying particular aspects of their emotional makeup.

In such groups, God has been able to speak to me through other group members who prayed for me by name each day, listened to me, and questioned me as I shared what I was discovering about myself. The groups not only have encouraged me, but have held me accountable for acting on what God showed me. They have been a mirror that allowed me to face myself and the emotional dimension of my HEART.

As I have subjected myself to the discipline and process that Christ uses to order, heal, and develop dimensions of emotional life, I have discovered an amazing resource for the church in the high-tech age. For it is out of my own emotional growth that I am able to obey more effectively what Jesus commands for the HEART—to love God, myself, and the people around me.

6. The Ethical Dimension

Welcome to the strange and unusual world of the ethical dimension of the HEART. I say unusual because quite honestly I did not know before I researched the biblical HEART that it *had* an ethical dimension. And I call it strange because of the odd and strikingly incongruous interpretation of ethics I occasionally encounter in pockets of the Christian community, where "Christian ethics" appear to be an attempt to repackage personal prejudices or biases.

From the viewpoint of the HEART, "ethics" refers simply to the knowledge of good and evil. Several years ago, after a Sunday-morning class in which I made this point, a bright young Christian businessman came up to talk about what I had said. He thought that in talking about good and evil I was three levels above where most people are living.

He said that when people must make a business or personal decision, the first question they ask is, "Do I or don't I want to do it?"—not "Is it good or evil?" If they get to the next level, they may ask whether it is legal or illegal. At the third level, they may ask whether it is right or wrong as judged by friends and peers. Only at the fourth and highest level would the question arise of good or evil as judged by God. And the young man didn't think most people ever get to that level.

He may be right. People seem to have a very difficult time confronting life's issues in terms of good and evil. When I say "good or evil," I am not talking about abstract concepts, any more than I am talking about ethics as an academic course of study. By ethics I mean a discipline of the HEART, a way of making decisions based on the reality of good and evil in the world around us and in our own lives. We choose one action over another according to the condition of our HEARTs.

For lay men and women who must live out their faith in the world, decisions that depend on ethics cannot be avoided. We are constantly faced with situations in which we must choose what to do. And we make those decisions out of the ethical dimension of our HEARTs.

A TRAVELING SALESMAN STORY

I talked recently with a high-tech sales executive, who recounted a story about a trip he made to Germany to visit the manufacturer of equipment he sold in the United States. There he encountered a number of situations that clearly challenged him in the ethical dimension of his HEART.

After a day at the factory, this salesman was taken to dinner by a local executive. On the way to the restaurant, the German host discovered that my friend owned a German car. He ordered the limousine to stop and disappeared into a store, returning with a car stereo costing over two thousand dollars. He presented the stereo to the American salesman as a gift! Then they proceeded on to the restaurant for dinner.

After dinner, the German executive (who was known throughout German industry as a champion beer drinker), coaxed my friend into one of his famous "drink-you-under-the-table" beer drinking contests. The drinking contest lasted for several hours, and the American managed to stay in the contest only because he took up with a waitress and had her water his beer. When the evening ended, the American was pretty well smashed but still on his feet, and the German executive was angry because his opponent had not passed out.

The American stumbled back to his hotel on foot to get some fresh air. Thirty minutes later there was a knock at the door. The waitress from the restaurant was standing there. She spoke little English and he spoke no German, but it was pretty clear why she had come. After some fumbling attempts at conversation, he sent her on her way, and her parting comment in broken English was "Next time spend night together."

Is this just another "traveling salesman" story? Perhaps, but it is also an example of the kind of ethical decisions ordinary Christians may encounter in the high-tech world around them. To put the story in proper perspective, the American claimed to be a practicing Christian. How did he make the decisions he did?

He probably considered all the questions mentioned by my young businessman friend after that Sunday-morning class: He certainly had to weigh whether he *wanted* to take a certain action or not. There was a question whether some of the situations confronting him were legal or illegal. The man's family, friends, and co-workers certainly would have an opinion as to whether the proposed actions were right or wrong. But when it came down to actually making the decisions, this man had to rely on his HEART's ability to discern good and evil.

ETHICS—A MATTER OF THE HEART

It is at the level of the ethical dimension of the HEART that events like these are examined as to whether they are good or evil. And again, it's a matter of choosing one or the other, not just assigning abstract labels. Is the beer-drinking bout an example of the use of drugs in business or symptomatic of alcoholism in industry? At a time when the *Wall Street Journal* calls a one-hundred-fifty-dollar gift excessive, is a two-thousand-dollar gift a bribe? Was the visit of the waitress to the American's hotel room a use of prostitution for business purposes? We can weigh these questions calmly and make judgments about them, but for my salesman friend each represented a situation in which he had to act—one way or another.

If I examine events like these as abstract case studies of ethics, I miss the point of an ethical dimension of the

HEART. The challenge is not to discern good and evil in the world around me so that I can judge others. The true challenge is to discern good and evil because God holds me accountable for my own choices.

As a follower of Jesus Christ, I am not perfect, but I am responsible. My interior strategy must include development of the ethical dimension of my HEART. And this requires far more than rolling through life like a pinball in a pinball machine, trying to hit as many of the "good" buttons as I can and avoid the "evil" buttons, while God rings up the score.

Biblical examples dealing with the ethical dimension of the HEART shift the struggle of good with evil away from exterior issues dealing with life out in the world. They make it very clear that ethics first of all is a matter of what is *inside*. And they picture the HEART as having three important characteristics that pertain to the ethical dimension: momentum, polarity, and the ability to accumulate either good or evil.

MOMENTUM, POLARITY, AND ACCUMULATION

Momentum describes the tendency of anything that starts moving in a particular direction to keep on moving in the same direction. Early one summer morning in Fredricksburg, Texas, I saw two men who had just performed an unwitting demonstration of this principle. A soft-drink delivery truck was parked at the curb, and the two men were out in the intersection, sweeping up broken glass and picking up smashed soft-drink cases. They told me that the driver had been going too fast when he turned the corner. And the cases of drinks, which had developed momentum in the direction the truck was originally going, had kept on going straight—right out of the bed of the truck and into the intersection. The HEART has that kind of momentum; once it starts toward good or evil, it keeps going in the direction in which it started. And the direction of movement of the HEART is chosen by the individual.

The HEART also has the tendency to develop *polarity* — a "tilt" toward good or evil. Once this polarity develops, the HEART's momentum will cause it to continue "leaning" in the direction it has become polarized.

A third characteristic of the ethical dimension of the HEART is *accumulation.* I recall a university student who encountered the claims of Jesus and, on the spot, committed his life to Christ. He returned to his usual routine in the dorm, classroom, and social life. After a few weeks, he met with his Christian counselor, who asked him how things were going. He said, "It's like there is a black dog and a white dog inside my life and they are fighting all the time." The counselor asked him which one was winning. The student thought a moment and replied matter-of-factly, "The one I feed the most."

What the student was describing was the tendency of the HEART to accumulate good or evil according to what is put into it. The HEART does not encounter good or evil and merely bounce off and go on its way unchanged; it builds up good or evil with each encounter. This is what continually causes the HEART to become polarized and gain momentum either toward good or evil. An effective interior strategy must focus on the correct "feeding" of the HEART to build polarity and momentum toward good.

AN INVENTORY OF GOOD AND EVIL

An interior strategy must also provide a way to take inventory of the good and evil that have accumulated in the HEART. Jesus used fruit trees as an example of how we can do this: "Either make the tree good, and its fruit good; or make the tree bad, and its fruit bad; for the tree is known by its fruit" (Matt. 12:33).

This example is very meaningful to me, because our old homeplace in Oklahoma had a small orchard. Even today, I can give you a report on the trees because, as a child, I knew the quality of fruit each tree produced. The cherries were great; the pears and apples were fair; and the peaches and apricots were terrible. In the same way, Jesus said, it is possible to tell what the HEART has accumulated by the fruit it produces!

Jesus went on to say that our *speech* is a telltale indicator of what is in the HEART: "How can you speak good, when you are evil? For out of the abundance of the HEART the mouth speaks. The good man out of his good treasure brings forth good, and the evil man out of his evil treasure brings forth evil. I tell you, on the day of judgment men will render account for every careless word they utter; for by your words you will be justified, and by your words you will be condemned" (Matt. 12:34–37).

Recently, I met the chairman of the board of a large corporation, who informed me that he never allows profanity to be used in his presence at work. I appreciate his sincere effort to witness to his faith in his business, but I don't believe that when he meets Christ face to face at the judgment he will have to account for all the profanity uttered in his presence! In fact, I don't think clean or dirty speech is what Jesus was talking about here. What he was saying was that our words make a difference because they reflect the good and evil that have accumulated in our HEARTs.

A CONVERSATION FROM THE HEART

One Monday night during the summer, I flew to Los Angeles for a consultation with a client in Pasadena. I am a nonsmoker with sinus and allergy problems that are irritated by any kind of smoke, so I had made sure my seat was right in the center of the NO SMOKING section. I got out a Bible and my notes to prepare a lecture on (what else?) developing the HEART.

Half an hour passed before the woman in the next seat fired up a cigarette. My first thought was to hit the stewardess's call button and ask loudly, "I'm not in the SMOKING section, am I?"

This response, I'm ashamed to say, would have been straight from the HEART. I have the natural tendency to be nasty and petty when my rights are violated, especially when I'm traveling. But fortunately, my HEART is also in the process of being transformed by Jesus Christ. So I was able to chuckle over the momentum of my own HEART, pray silently for grace, and go to Plan B—keeping my mouth shut.

When the flight attendant came with the meal, she said, "You both know this is a NO SMOKING section, don't you?" The woman next to me looked terribly embarrassed and apologized, saying that she had requested a SMOKING seat. Seeing the mortified look on her face, I was glad I had kept my mouth shut.

As the meal service continued, we started to talk. She glanced over at my Bible as she said, "I'm an engineer with —— [she named a prominent company in the southeast] and I didn't really want to make this trip. My son is getting married Friday, and I need to be home, but my boss told me I had to go. I also have a fourteen year old daughter who always stays with a friend when I travel. (My friend and I are both divorced.) But this friend just let a man move in with her, and I'm not about to let my daughter stay with her now."

We talked over dinner about her job pressures, the grief over losing a friend, and the stress of the upcoming wedding. I explained that I was researching a talk on ideas that would help people like us cope with this kind of stress in our high-technology world.

At this, she perked up and volunteered: "At my company I have developed a method of approaching my job which makes some people think I am a leadership wizard."

I asked her to explain.

"Well, I get up every morning, and I ask God to show me what I am supposed to do for that day. Then I do it. At night, when I go home, I thank God for the day and I go to bed and sleep real good."

I told her I thought she had hit on a great method. And I asked her where she had learned it or how she had thought it up. She looked a little embarrassed, then she finally said, "I am in Alcoholics Anonymous. I'm an alcoholic. That's where I got it." She went on to tell me how much AA had helped her in the practice of her faith.

As the plane landed in Los Angeles, my seatmate said, "I want to thank you for being so kind and not saying anything when I was smoking in the NO SMOKING section." And I winced inwardly, aware of how close I had come to letting my "black dog" take a bite out of her. But I celebrated the fact that God is using my interior strategy to pull the polarity of my HEART toward the good.

In my traveling companion I sensed a common bond, which I believe can be traced to the ethical dimension of the HEART. When we discussed alcohol dependency, stress on the job, and sexual relations outside marriage, both of us assumed that these were decisions made at the level of the HEART. We both knew that the HEART can accumulate evil, become polarized and build momentum in that direction, but that God's power and a certain amount of personal discipline could turn a HEART toward the good.

ACCOUNTABLE FOR WHAT GOES IN

When Jesus spoke to the multitude about the treasure of the HEART ("For where your treasure is, there will your HEART be also," Luke 12:34), he was underscoring the fact that we are accountable for what we allow to accumulate in our HEARTs.

A high-tech analogy of this is the computer. Anyone who has programming experience knows that the computer is a glorified idiot that does exactly what you tell it. If Moses had had a computer, there would have been an eleventh commandment: "Garbage in—garbage out!" A computer cannot compensate for faulty programs and bad data fed to it. Neither can the HEART.

What is at stake is much more than God's keeping a list of evil deeds. The real issue is whether the momentum of our HEARTs aims us to a deeper relationship with God, the significant people in our lives, ourselves, and the world around us—or whether we are propelled into a fragmented world of broken relationships.

Jesus spoke directly to this issue with his parable of the sower (Luke 8:5–15). The "seed" mentioned in the parable is the Word of God, which meets various fates as it tries to make its way to the HEART. There is no better tactic for developing the ethical dimension of the HEART than "sowing" it with the Word of God.

But a major counterattack comes from the Evil One, who

disarms the Word of God so that the HEART may accumulate evil. "And as for what fell among the thorns, they are those who hear, but as they go on their way they are choked by the cares and riches and pleasures of life, and their fruit does not mature" (Luke 8:14).

SATAN'S STRATEGY IN THE HIGH-TECH AGE

The devil's strategy to choke the HEART with evil has never been more effective than in the high-tech age. Stress has become a status symbol, and the affluence and prosperity of our high-tech society can easily choke a HEART with nonproductive cares, pleasures, and riches. The HEART is left ethically stunted and underdeveloped, blinded to the evil it has accumulated in the form of objects and activities that are neutral in themselves but evil in obsessive excess.

As a high-technology entrepreneur, I live in a world where the risks—and the potential material rewards—are enormous. I have met entrepreneurs who have bet everything on one significant achievement—one chance to grab the gold ring. I have also met venture capitalists who, on the surface, look like wise investment bankers, but who really are more like Las Vegas gamblers with M.B.A.s and pin-striped suits. And I have also come to realize that the road to entrepreneurial success is covered with the bodies of people whose lives disintegrated because they could not handle failure or were overwhelmed by success.

There is no safe place out in the high-tech world. Safety comes with a HEART that has developed its ethical dimension by accumulating good—by polarizing and building momentum toward good. Jesus summed it up in the story of the sower: "And as for that in the good soil, they are those who, hearing the word, hold it fast in an honest and good HEART, and bring forth fruit with patience" (Luke 8:15).

A GOAL OF PURITY

What, then, is a goal for developing the ethical dimension of the HEART? At times, I worry about my own ability to maintain balance in the high-tech entrepreneurial environment. For me, the goal must not be just something to shoot for when I am in a mood to impress God. It cannot be optional, because it is the means by which I keep my HEART from choking on evil!

I believe the goal can be found in one of the Beatitudes: "Blessed are the pure in HEART, for they shall see God" (Matt. 5:8). The goal for the ethical dimension is purity of HEART.

Now, if this were a goal I must reach on my own, the situation would be hopeless. As a once-a-year recreational skier, I would have a far better chance at an Olympic gold medal in the downhill event. I cannot purify my HEART by polarizing it toward good and overcoming evil all by myself.

But I believe Christ had something in mind which is more profound than a pull-yourself-up-by-the-bootstraps remodeling of the HEART. When he said, "Blessed are the pure in HEART, for they shall see God," he was simply stating the effect of the Spirit's work in the human HEART. The pure in HEART will see God—and see him very often. It is the daily guidance of the Spirit that gives me the power and discernment to sort the good from the evil as I decide what goes into my HEART.

My hope as I follow Jesus Christ into the high-tech age is Christ's promise that I will see God moment by moment. By his power, I am able to keep my HEART from choking on evil and keep it moving toward the goal of a pure HEART. The pure in HEART will be blessed by God's practical guidance through all the flash and glitter of the high-tech age.

As the ethical dimension of my HEART develops, I will be able to filter all I perceive in the world around me. This is the means by which I see my high-tech world through Christ's eyes. With his eyes I will not only see the good and evil in my world; I will be able to sort the good and the evil in my own life. And as God changes my HEART, my world will change, too.

7. The Intellectual Dimension

Bumper stickers are just about the only pleasures left in driving the clogged freeway that connects my Dallas neighborhood to the rest of the world. These little messages give satisfaction to their owners and provide me with a source of amusement as I creep along in traffic. (I do have to admit that, faced with seventy-five thousand cars per day over the freeway's designed capacity, I find myself really appreciating the one that growls, "Welcome to Texas! Now go home.")

Recently, however, I saw a bumper sticker that bothered me. It proclaimed, "God said it. I believe it. That settles it." The more I think about that message, the more disturbing I find it.

I hope that bumper sticker is only a rather terse way of stating that someone found his or her way to God. If that's the case, I agree—the death and resurrection of Jesus certainly does settle the future for those who believe in him. But what bothers me is the feeling that the bumper sticker is really saying, "I've come this far, and this is where I stop. I am set for eternity, and I am signing off *until* the next life." To me, it implies that being a Christian means completely shutting down the intellectual dimension of life. And nothing could be more alien to the biblical concept of HEART as I have come to understand it.

HEART AND HEAD

There is a lot about the Christian life that is unsettling if we are used to thinking in the world's terms. Obedience to Jesus Christ is unsettling. Developing the HEART is unsettling. And the idea that there is an intellectual dimension to the HEART can also be unsettling—especially since most of us are used to thinking of "heart" and "head" as opposites! This view that the intellect is the opposite of the HEART is so widespread in our culture that it is hard to avoid. The modern industrial psychologists who have analyzed high-tech society and issued a serious plea for leaders to "develop their hearts as well as their heads" fall into the familiar "heart vs. head" trap. So did a friend of mine (a very knowledgeable scholar in the area of lay ministry) who followed my early progress on this book. He warned me not to let Christians forget that the intellect must be developed "as well as" the HEART.

In fact, when I first started putting this book together, I went along with this popular way of thinking. I even included a separate section on "development of the head" in an early draft of the manuscript. But as I continued to research the biblical concept of the HEART, I realized that the biblical idea of HEART *includes* the head—in contrast to the more common opposition of "head" and "heart." The Hebrews neatly folded the intellect into their concept of the HEART. And this concept permeates both the Old and New Testaments.

A CALL TO DEVELOP THE INTELLECT

When the Scriptures are read with the Hebrew definition of the HEART in mind, some significant facts emerge. One is that people who "give their hearts to Jesus" in an emotional, moving moment must face the requirement that their heads are included in that commitment! A call is heard throughout the Bible to develop the intellect as an act of obedience to God.

Development of the intellectual dimension of the HEART is a fresh challenge for the laity who must live in our high-tech society. In the past, some churches have recognized a call to intellectual development but have tended to reserve it for seminarians and for Christian scholars such as C. S.

Lewis. At the other end of the spectrum are Christian traditions that have displayed an anti-intellectual bias based on the mistaken notion that thinking will get you into trouble every time. (Their bumper sticker reads, "God said it. I believe it. That settles it. Now forget it!") This anti-intellectual bias has not been helped by theologically arrogant scholars who parade before the public with ideas and causes that to the people in the pews seem controversial, bizarre, or irrelevant.

At the center of the church today are the ordinary Christians who must heed this call to develop the intellectual dimension in order to have an impact for Jesus Christ in the world. Some futurologists predict that the next phase of the high-tech age will be the age of information. With the explosive proliferation of computers, telecommunications, and video and audio broadcasting, people today already have far more information than they can convert into knowledge. I believe the task falls to the laity to blend the information explosion of the high-tech age with the information found in God's Word in order to come up with a practical guide for personal survival, ministry, and the living of a meaningful life in a high-tech society.

BASIC TOOLS OF THE INTELLECTUAL DIMENSION

The first step in developing the intellectual dimension is to put into perspective the concept of "the mind," which appears in many places in the biblical text. Remember, the Hebrews were not as category-minded as we tend to be today. The biblical words translated into English as "mind" could also be translated as referring to the intellectual dimension of the HEART.

When I talk about my "mind," I must include my collection of mental aptitudes—God-given abilities that are the mental tools I am born with. I can develop these aptitudes and train myself to use them, but essentially they are gifts. And most people have stronger aptitudes in one or two areas than in others.

Two examples of mental aptitudes are word memory and

number memory. (In school, the "smart kids" are often those with these aptitudes, which enable them to parrot back material on exams.) Another example is convergent thinking of both the analytical and diagnostic kinds. The ability to crank through equations to a solution (analytical thinking) and the ability to organize scattered and unrelated data to come up with an insightful description (diagnostic thinking) are valuable gifts that can be sharpened with training and practice. So are the creative aptitudes, such as the ability to plan into the future (foresight) or to produce new ideas rapidly (ideaphoria).

This collection of mental aptitudes makes up what we call the mind. Each person starts out with a given set of mental tools. The first step in developing the intellectual dimension of the HEART is *acceptance of this set of mental tools as a gift from God.* Development and use of the contents of the mental tool box is an act of stewardship—God cannot use an empty head!

BUILDING A SPIRITUAL IQ

Mental aptitudes are combined with experience and training to develop an intellectual capability, which is sometimes measured by an IQ (intelligence quotient) test. Two people with the same aptitudes may have very different IQ scores because IQ measures the collection of concepts and ideas that are learned and retained.

It has been shown that IQ scores are related directly to the size of a person's vocabulary, and that IQ scores can be improved by increasing vocabulary. In other words, IQ tests reflect *education* as well as native ability. And this is an important point when it comes to developing the intellectual dimension of the HEART. The call to develop this dimension is a call to increase the spiritual IQ—to develop God-given mental abilities and accumulate spiritual concepts and ideas. This means working long and hard to get *spiritually educated.*

But what does it mean to be an educated person? Am I educated because I have degrees in engineering and a doctorate in atomic physics? Or do these certificates merely

100

indicate that I am technically trained at a very high level?

Opinions differ on just what education means. Ask one person where he was educated, and he may tell you the high school or university he attended. Ask someone else the same question, and you may hear tales of time spent in New York or Rome or London or Paris with exposure to social and cultural advantages. And both explanations are valid. Formal teaching is valuable. But exposure to the "finer things" in the real world is an enriching educational experience no school can give.

A growing HEART must be exposed to spiritual "advantages" as well. To be educated, the HEART must be confronted with knowledge of God's impact on human history, God's impact on human life today, and God's potential impact on the future.

SWIMMING AGAINST THE STREAM

Although there is a great gulf in time between the high-tech age and the golden age of Greece, Socrates faced this same task of defining an educated person. His list of characteristics included the description, "one who controls his environment rather than being controlled by it." In the high-tech society, my character is continuously shaped and reshaped by the pounding hammers of corporate, financial, educational, and governmental institutions. The challenge to develop the HEART includes developing the strength to resist the blows of the institutional hammers. Christ calls me to rise to the point that I can exercise enough force of character to reshape these institutions of the high-tech age rather than being shaped by them.

Institutional renewal can be a lonely countercultural venture full of risk and difficulty. It takes a developed HEART to swim upstream. Yet, that is the tradition that we as Christians carry into this high-tech age. The apostle Paul launched one of the great cultural challenges in recorded history as he sailed for Rome, ready to take on the Roman Empire at its peak of world power and influence.

A decade ago, I retraced Paul's steps through the streets

of Rome and found myself on a hill overlooking the Roman Forum. The ruins of markets and pagan temples still reflect the awesome glory that once was Rome. What a place for a traveling Jewish tentmaker to sell his idea that an Israeli carpenter was raised from the dead and outranked the Roman emperor!

Long before Paul set foot in Rome, he revealed his strategy to the church at Rome: "Therefore, my brothers, I implore you by God's mercy to offer your very selves to him; a living sacrifice, dedicated and fit for his acceptance, the worship offered by mind and HEART" (Rom. 12:1, NEB). Paul's plan focused on the worship of God with commitment of the whole HEART. Phillips in his translation continues, "Don't let the world around you squeeze you into its own mold, . . . so that you may prove in practice that the plan of God for you is good, meets all his demands and moves toward the goal of true maturity" (Rom. 12:2–3, PHILLIPS).

Paul raised the goal from becoming an educated person to becoming a *mature* educated person. This is the call for developing the intellectual dimension of the HEART. This is also the key to freedom from the pressure of the world's mold.

WHAT DO I DO WITH GOD?

In the Bible, the intellectual dimension of the HEART surfaces when people find themselves in an intense struggle to figure out what to do with God. The Gospels are full of the stories of people who were confronted with a Man unlike anyone they had ever encountered and who were forced to use their intellects to try to figure out this Person who stood before them.

Mark, in his Gospel, records the story of a paralyzed man brought to Christ by his hopeful friends (2:1–12). They peeled off a roof tile and lowered him down so he could be physically healed. But before healing the man of paralysis, Jesus said to the man, "My son, your sins are forgiven."

This really floored the scribes who were sitting in the room; the Gospel writer says that they began "questioning in their HEARTs." Who was this man? Only God could forgive sins; who did this man Jesus think he was? Faced with a Person who claimed to forgive sins and was able to heal a man of physical affliction, the scribes had to stretch their intellects, to process the data, to try to figure out whom they were dealing with—a blasphemer or God.

Nicodemus is another example of a person who had to struggle intellectually to understand the reality of Christ. Nicodemus knew there was something special about Jesus; that is why he went to talk to him. But then Jesus started talking in seemingly absurd terms, saying things like, "Unless one is born anew, he cannot see the kingdom of God." Nicodemus was perplexed; he asked, "How can a man be born when he is old?" he asked. And Jesus' answer indicated that Nicodemus needed to grow in the intellectual dimension of his HEART: "Truly, truly, I say to you, unless one is born of water and the Spirit, he cannot enter the kingdom of God. . . . Are you a teacher of Israel, and yet you do not understand this? . . . If I have told you earthly things and you do not believe, how can you believe if I tell you heavenly things?" (John 3:1–21).

Even those closest to Jesus had to stretch the intellectual dimension of their HEARTs in order to figure out who had broken into their lives. In fact, sometimes those who were closest had the most difficulty understanding. After the crucifixion, Jesus' followers were devastated. Their whole religious enterprise had crashed with the death of their leader, and they could not understand why this had happened. So when two followers of Jesus were joined by a stranger on the road to Emmaus, the "candid camera" was in place to catch one of history's most embarrassing moments.

These two men could tell that the stranger hadn't been in the area long, because he didn't seem to know what had been going on in Jerusalem. So they filled him in on the crucifixion of Jesus, their great leader, who had bombed out and been killed. And then they looked Christ right in the eye without recognizing him and made a real blooper: "We had hoped he was the one." Oooops!

Jesus replied then, "Oh foolish men, and slow of HEART

103

to believe all that the prophets had spoken!" Here he was referring to the intellectual dimension of the HEART. Intellectually, the disciples had not grasped what the prophets had written about the Christ who was to enter history, experience death, and stand before them as the risen Christ. And even when their risen Lord was walking right beside them, their minds couldn't stretch enough to comprehend!

From the very beginning of his time on earth, Jesus stretched the minds of those he encountered. And some seemed to accept the reality of who he was more easily than others. The shepherds got the word of his birth by means of an angel who appeared in a spectacular presentation complete with background music—"to you is born . . . City of David . . . a Savior." And I find it interesting that they did not say, "This is kind of weird; let's just sit here and see if anything else happens before we take off. It might be a false alarm." The shepherds just moved out, showed up, told their story; they were sold on the program.

But the one person who quietly wondered what was actually taking place was Jesus' own mother. Mary was trying to make sense out of what had happened in her life. Who was this child? What was he about? Was all this real? "But Mary kept all these things, pondering them in her HEART" (Luke 2:1–19).

When people are questioning in their HEARTs, considering in their HEARTs, pondering in their HEARTs, their best intellectual abilities are at work on the questions, "Is God real in my life?" and "What am I going to do about it?" The intellectual dimension of the HEART must guide these decisions.

CALL FOR AN UNDERSTANDING HEART

When I set out to develop the intellectual dimension of the HEART, what goal could I have that speaks to the unfolding drama of the high-tech age?

Jesus frequently spoke in parables, even though throughout most of his ministry he was speaking to the most religiously literate people on earth at that time. The Jewish people had a wealth of information supplied by rabbis and priests and woven into elaborate national feasts, rituals, and holidays.

The disciples finally came to Jesus and asked a good question, "Why do you speak to them in parables?" Jesus explained, "This is why I speak to them in parables, because seeing they do not see, and hearing they do not hear, nor do they understand" (Matt. 13:10–16).

No one people in the history of the human race had more information on the Lord God of the universe and his desires for his people than did the Jewish people. Yet, Jesus claimed that at that moment they did not have what it took to understand the secrets of the kingdom of heaven! This is a dramatic case of information without knowledge.

The prophecy of Isaiah, which Jesus claims these people had fulfilled, spells it out: "You shall indeed hear but never understand, and you shall indeed see but never perceive. For this people's HEART has grown dull, and their ears are heavy of hearing, and their eyes they have closed, lest they should perceive with their eyes, and hear with their ears, and understand with their HEART, and turn for me to heal them" (Isa. 6:9–10).

This quote from Isaiah holds the key to both the negative and positive aspects of the HEART's intellectual dimension. When the HEART swings negative, it is described here as dull. A dull HEART faces a wealth of information but comes up with nothing in the way of knowledge or insight. It grapples with the available data and draws a blank. A dull HEART cannot see what God is trying to reveal or hear what God is trying to say. The people whom Jesus called dull-HEARTed were dulled as individuals and as a community. With all their history and background, they were still missing the message, even when they got it from Jesus face to face.

The goal of developing the intellectual dimension is *an understanding HEART*—one which converts information *from* God and *about* God into knowledge *of* God, so that I can see his way and hear what he is saying to me. With an understanding HEART, I am able to see myself and my world from God's perspective.

The opposite of this is a dull HEART, which breaks my relationship with God and sets me on a search for healing and fulfillment in a high-technology world that ultimately holds no hope for either. Healing comes when, with an understanding HEART, I see my own brokenness and turn to God for healing. Healing and wholeness will forever elude those who are dull of HEART.

A few years back, E. V. Hill, who is pastor of a black congregation in the Watts area of Los Angeles, visited the congregation of which I am a member. The purpose of his visit was to help us look at what God would have us do in the inner city and ghettos of Dallas. But he also pointed out some interesting characteristics of a black church meeting. For instance, a black congregation gives help to the preacher; when the preacher does well, they shout, "Praise the Lord! Amen!" and when he does poorly, they say, "Help him Lord, Help him!" In turn, the preacher comes up with what are called "shouting verses"—Scripture passages turned into the simplest, strongest, most positive statements possible.

I have never spoken to a black congregation, but I learned enough from E. V. Hill to construct a shouting verse out of Isaiah's prophecy. "If I have eyes to see and perceive, if I have ears to hear, and if I have a HEART to understand, I can turn to God and be healed!" When I develop an understanding heart, I can experience healing in my relationship with God, myself, and the significant other people in my life. And when that happens, even a reserved, orderly Presbyterian can shout, "Amen! Praise God!"

First must come healing in my relationship with God. The understanding HEART is a HEART that is open to Jesus Christ. The death and resurrection of Jesus heals the break between me and God when I accept it with my mind and claim it in my life. Healing occurs as I experience the love of God and am able to return that love.

GOD THINKS I'M REAL

I have a history of being dull-HEARTed when it comes to the love of God and love for God. But I have made some progress toward understanding the love of God through a modern parable. Although I have heard this story told about a variety of places, I like to imagine it taking place in one of my favorite settings—the Stagecoach Inn in Salado, Texas.

Stagecoach Inn was once an overnight stop for the Butterfield Stage, but now it houses one of the best restaurants in central Texas—a favorite with families. The long-time waitresses recite the menu, which changes every day and is never written down: "Today we have roast beef, chicken fried steak, and so on. . . ."

One day a small boy was at the restaurant with his family. He listened to the list the waitress recited, but didn't hear his favorite. So when the waitress asked for his order, he popped up with, "I'd like a hot dog!"

His mother smoothly inserted, "He will have the roast beef with mashed potatoes."

The elderly waitress continued to look the boy right in the eye and asked, "What do you want on your hot dog?"

"Mustard!" shot back the answer.

As the waitress disappeared into the kitchen, the boy sat still and quiet for a few moments, deep in thought. He finally tugged on his mother's arm and said, "Mommy, that lady thinks I'm *real.*"

In this story, I found a key to the love of God. When God looks at me, he sees me as a real person. He takes me seriously.

But the story can be turned around. For me to love God means I must think God is real. To love God, I must take Christ seriously as a person. I must work at developing a relationship. As the dullness of my HEART wears away and my HEART develops understanding, I see the Lord God revealed. And I show my love by obedience to Jesus Christ in all areas of my life.

An understanding HEART will allow me to see the world around me from Christ's perspective. This happens when I communicate with God person to person in all of the five areas of the HEART. The intellectual dimension can never be isolated from the other four when I deal directly with God.

OVERCOMING DULLNESS OF HEART

In the high-tech age, it is particularly important to overcome dullness of HEART in the area of work and labor in the world. This is one area where there is a shortage of genuine heroes—men and women who have developed the intellectual dimension of the HEART to achieve true understanding of the Lord God and his creative work in the world and in their own lives.

An example of such a hero is the Swiss physician, Paul Tournier. As the life-changing power of Jesus Christ touched his life and work, Dr. Tournier joined in founding a medical fellowship committed to "medicine of the whole person"—healing people spiritually and emotionally as well as physically.

In his first book to be translated into English, *The Doctor's Case Book in the Light of the Bible,*[1] Tournier speaks to a major issue of the high-tech age—a HEART dulled by technology. What happens, says Dr. Tournier, is that people lose responsibility for their own destiny.

In medicine, the effect of such dullness of HEART is to convert sickness into a fantasy epic—a battle scene between the "good guys" who fight for health and wellness and the "bad guys" who represent illness and disease. Dr. Tournier's description makes me think of a scene from the movie, *Star Wars,* in which valiant heroes rely on "The Force" to battle treacherous villains in a cosmic setting.

In such a model, the feared "bad guys" are the things that can destroy me. Bacteria, viruses, hereditary weaknesses, psychological complexes, chemical affinities and addictions, or the "disease of the month" (cancer, herpes, AIDS, etc.) are my attackers. On the side of "good guys" are my protectors, who fight for my survival—disinfectants, intravenous injections, physical therapy, psychological therapy, X-rays, radiation, chemotherapy, CAT scans, NMR imaging, and so on.

---

1. New York: Harper, 1954.

Tournier says that the great tragedy of modern medicine comes when the patient begins to see himself as the battleground rather than a participant in the battle. The patient checks in the hospital and the fighting begins—with an attack by the bad guys, followed by counterattacks by the good guys. Meanwhile, the patient lies there passively watching the battle and awaiting its outcome to find out if he is dead or alive.

Medicine provides a dramatic example of dullness of HEART, but there are countless examples in the high-tech world. If it is on the computer, we think, we must believe it. If someone can get the broadcast into our living rooms, we must watch and listen. If chemists can grow or make it, we must smoke it, sniff it, drink it, swallow it, inject it, or rub it on. If manufacturers can produce it, we must buy it.

The heart dulled by technology loses responsibility for its own destiny. Unfortunately, this truth often applies to Christians who have allowed the intellectual dimension of the HEART to atrophy or remain undeveloped. Only when we work long and hard to develop an understanding HEART can we effectively reverse this trend.

Dr. Tournier tells of a visit he made to a friend who also practices medicine of the whole person in Florence, Italy. On hospital rounds, they visited an old woman who was apparently dying of a heart condition. The woman had been from doctor to doctor and had been treated by all the modern cardiac stimulants.

Tournier describes the scene:

My colleague leaned over her and said gently, "My dear, you must not only rely on medicine. There is yourself first, and God, and only after that the doctors." I saw in him the man of the people that he is, who knew how to talk to this woman of the people, recalling her to those basic truths whose importance is as great as ever in medicine, in spite of all our technical progress.

The patient looked in astonishment at this doctor, the first one to treat her as a person and not only as a case of heart trouble. She began to wake out of her passivity, to become once more aware of the part that she has to play in the struggle; she was becoming a person again.

The message conveyed by Dr. Tournier's colleague is the message that comes from an understanding HEART: "I know and understand God and the world he has created—technology and all. I know God takes you and your needs seriously. I know God thinks you are real. If you learn to tap your own power and God's power your life can be different."

Each person who develops the intellectual dimension in harmony with the other four dimensions of the HEART can carry this message of hope to the people who are seeing their worth as persons being eroded daily by waves of high technology.

8. The Spiritual Dimension

The fifth dimension of the HEART, the spiritual dimension, is the most controversial among people outside the community of faith. But even secular observers of life in this high-tech society can spot the problem of spiritually underdeveloped lives.

Dr. Michael Maccoby concluded his study of high-tech managers with the observation that all two hundred fifty people studied were spiritually stunted (see chapter 3). To Dr. Maccoby and his team of secular psychologists, this problem appeared as a serious shortage of spiritual values. And in his book, *The Leader,* Dr. Maccoby prescribed a remedy which involved reading and study to recover or develop spiritual values.

I do not discount the importance of spiritual values for an individual or a community. But I believe the true problem in the high-tech age is not only the lack of spiritual values, but also the lack of contact with *spiritual reality*—especially the lack of an ongoing personal relationship with the Source of all spiritual reality. Disappearance of authentic spiritual values is a symptom of this more fundamental problem of ignoring or denying spiritual reality. And spiritual values disappear when this fundamental relationship is not present to energize the spiritual dimension of the HEART.

This is not just a matter of *recognizing* or acknowledging spiritual reality. It has always been possible to recognize the existence of spiritual reality while at the same time avoiding, ignoring, or even opposing God.

Dr. Robert Jastrow, space pioneer and professor of earth sciences at Dartmouth College, professes to be an agnostic.

111

But in a recent lecture on cosmology and the order of the universe, Dr. Jastrow emphasized that recent scientific discoveries indicate that there are spiritual forces at work in the universe that are beyond science itself.[1]

Like Jastrow, a growing number of people in the high-tech world are beginning to acknowledge the possibility of spiritual reality. But that is not the same thing as actually making contact! Merely acknowledging spiritual reality will not necessarily help develop a HEART that is mature in the spiritual dimension.

The biblical remedy for an underdeveloped spiritual dimension is a strong, positive personal relationship with Jesus Christ. When this relationship is strong, the spiritual dimension of the HEART comes alive. In some special instances, I have seen a transformation take place right before my eyes!

But the development of the spiritual dimension of the HEART is difficult in the high-tech age. There is continual pressure to portray spiritual reality as an illusion or to minimize its importance in our lives. A thoughtful interior strategy is needed, therefore, to strengthen the contact with God and move the HEART toward spiritual maturity.

The challenge of developing the HEART is to allow Jesus Christ to break into our world and lives. In the previous chapters, I have explored ways that this can happen in the volitional, emotional, intellectual, and ethical dimensions. The spiritual dimension returns to the personal relationship between a loving, caring God and each of us who agrees to follow Christ in the often-hostile environment of this world. I would like to suggest six practical disciplines that can be practiced daily to develop the relationship with God and strengthen the spiritual dimension of the HEART.

KEEPING IN TOUCH

During the recent Holy Year, I joined a group of Presbyterians who were guests of the Vatican for discussions on the ministry of the laity. Our hosts made sure that we visited

---

1. Isthmus Institute Lectures on Cosmology, 18 October 1985.

those historical sites in Rome which hold significance for every Christian. Eventually, we arrived at the Sistine Chapel.

Portrayed in Michelangelo's famous ceiling mural is the mighty arm of God with a finger extended to flash the spark of life into Adam's finger. My mind snapped a frame around those hands and scrawled across it in mental graffiti—*Keep in Touch!* (The idea was not original with me but was a flashback to the work of a clever poster artist somewhere back in the United States.)

For the laity who venture forth into the high-tech age, the call to develop the spiritual dimension of the HEART is a call to keep in touch with spiritual reality in a world where spiritual values and traditions alone are not enough.

Jesus frequently dealt with religious people who clung to spiritual traditions while their contact with spiritual reality was allowed to weaken and atrophy. His name for such people was "hypocrite" (see Matt. 15:1–9). At one point, Jesus was confronted by a group of Jewish leaders who hiked out from Jerusalem to where he was teaching. In a heated exchange, Jesus charged, "You hypocrites!" and then explained the charge by quoting the prophet Isaiah.

A hypocrite knows the correct words and right rituals to praise and honor God. Yet while the worship attendance and church activities continue, God's voice is no longer heard. What is heard instead are people's voices—not God's—spouting forth doctrines and traditions they made up themselves. The distinguishing characteristic of a hypocrite is a distant HEART—a HEART that has lost touch with God. Jesus says, "Their HEART is far from me" (Matt. 15:8).

I remember being in a Bible study group with a business consultant who was deeply troubled by the hypocrites he had met in the business community. In fact, he told me they had been major roadblocks to his opening his HEART to Christ. But I found that this concept of a "distant HEART" helped me understand how the people he was dealing with could be so active in the Dallas Christian community and, at the same time, be so out of touch with God.

The first discipline for developing the spiritual dimension

of the HEART, then, is making time to "keep in touch" daily. The spiritual dimension of my HEART develops when I come each day as a sinner saved by grace into the forgiving, renewing presence of Christ. Without this daily contact, I drift into the role of high-tech hypocrite.

If there is a single word to describe life as an ordinary Christian in a high-tech world, it is *captivating*. Each day, in work or play, I can be captivated by a computer problem, development of a new product, a new business venture, or attractive vacation and recreational opportunities that use high technology to carry me away to some distant port of call. A daily prayer of focus can invite Christ to break into the world that captivates my mind and emotions.

Whether my day begins in my own laboratory, in the space lab at Cal Tech, or in the midst of a critical business negotiation, my prayer focuses on my intention to be obedient to Christ in the single day that lies before me. I may or may not understand what will be required of me. But by means of this prayer I consciously acknowledge the energizing presence of God's spirit in my life. By keeping in the stream of the spirit, I remind myself that God is moving through the world in the high-tech age just as he has done throughout history. And if I am available, I can be a part of his work on earth.

SEEKING GOD'S GUIDANCE

When I enter a day in touch with God and commit myself to being available and obedient, I still need marching orders. Guidance for the day and for my life can be found through prayer.

Does this idea have appeal in a high-tech society? I found a moving example in the autobiography of Frits Philips, who recently retired as president of Philips of Holland, a world-class high-technology company with almost four hundred thousand employees and sales over sixteen billion dollars last year. (I told part of his story in chapter 4.)

In *45 Years With Philips*,[2] he includes a chapter entitled

---

2. Fredrik Philips, *45 Years With Philips* (Poole: Blandford Press, 1978).

"New Convictions," in which he tells of friends who invited him to visit them to discuss some topic having to do with faith. Now, "faith" was a fuzzy subject to Frits; at this point in life, a church wedding and having his children baptized had been enough for him. But eventually he and his wife accepted the invitation with a determination to be cheerful regardless of how grim the Christians were.

Frits was surprised and impressed with the cheerful people he met—people whose purpose seemed to be to bring a new spirit to all churches and into every sphere of life. What most impressed Philips was their banding together to live the Christian life without compromise. He described what he found:

> What these friends had to offer was very simple. This is what they said, "Praying is not just talking, but above all listening. God is ready to guide our thoughts if we give Him time to do it. The only condition is that we are prepared to carry out what He shows us. We should check the thoughts we get against standards which Jesus has shown in the Sermon on the Mount. Honesty, purity, unselfishness and love."
>
> We were deeply impressed. Could what our friends say really be true? If our creator could speak in our hearts in this twentieth century as He did the people in the Old and New Testament this would not only make people a lot happier but also could alter the world.

What captured Frits Philips's imagination for Jesus Christ is the second exercise for developing the spiritual dimension of the heart: seeking God's guidance, listening for a reply, and carrying out what he shows us. I have learned that there are no sacred or secular boundaries. God is interested in the concerns of the HEART as it touches any area of life. Once he gave his life to Christ, Philips continually sought God's guidance for the company he eventually headed as well as for his personal life and family life.

Philips perceived immediately how God speaks—directly to our HEARTs. As I seek God's guidance for the living of a single day and for direction in those "special" decisions of work, family, and church, God will speak to my intellect, my will, my ethics, my emotions, and the spiritual point

115

of contact I share with him. When I realize again and again that God loves me and is intimately concerned with even my day-to-day life, the spiritual dimension of the HEART builds strength and endurance for the long haul.

DISCIPLINE OF THE WORD

Last summer, I did some work in an optics laboratory that had a telephone with a defective earpiece. I could call people and talk to them, but I could not hear anything they said. This defective telephone receiver is a symbol of my typical prayer experience. I shout away at God, but my receiver is usually out of order.

For life in this high-tech age, I need guidance and direction from the Lord. And sometimes I have special questions that need special, specific answers. But the special questions such as where I shall live or work or worship or whom I shall marry comprise only a small percentage of the questions I face in day-to-day living!

James I. Packer, in his book, *Knowing God,*[3] estimates that only 15 percent of the questions we face in our lives are of the "special" type. The other 85 percent of the questions brought to God are more general in nature. The percentage may vary, of course, but the vast collection of these questions are already covered in the contents of the Old and New Testaments.

This brings us to the third exercise for developing the spiritual dimension—what I call "discipline of the word." This means taking time each day to listen to Scripture as God's guidance for my life in my faith, family, work, and life in the community where I live. I have discovered that the Bible is a book about relationships. I must turn to the Scriptures daily to understand what my relationships with God, myself, the significant people in my life, and with the world around me are supposed to look like in this high-tech age, where positive role models are scarce.

Some days, I manage to read a "full order" as prescribed

---

3. Downers Grove, IL: InterVarsity, 1973.

by the ancient "rule for the monastery"—one chapter of the Old Testament and one-half chapter of the New. Sometimes, I cover a little more or less. Often I turn for help to devotional guides, such as Oswald Chamber's classic, *My Utmost for His Highest.* [4] Exactly what I read is less important than the fact that my life must be bounded and shaped by the word of God, not the word of the high-tech age.

MEDITATION OVER SCRIPTURE

In my work and ministry, I must work and struggle to be obedient to Jesus Christ. I find that I need something more than guidance for the special vocational questions, and I need more than a general knowledge of God's guidelines. I need God to penetrate my HEART and reshape my life. To do this, God works through the fourth exercise—meditation over Scripture.

Spiritual reality brings the discipline of a loving God transforming a human life. Moses cautioned the children of God to "know then in your HEART that, as a man disciplines his son, the Lord your God disciplines you" (Deut. 8:5). The author of the book of Hebrews points out, "For the moment all discipline seems painful rather than pleasant; later it yields the peaceful fruit of righteousness to those who have been trained by it" (Heb. 12:11).

The result of discipline is righteousness, which throughout the Old and New Testament can be translated "right relationships." In a high-tech age characterized by broken relationships, the discipline of God's Word offers me the hope of getting my act together.

In meditation over Scripture, I turn to God's Word with the prayer of the Psalmist, "Search me, O Lord, and know my HEART." I first read a passage and center in on a few verses, a phrase, or even a single word. After I reread the passage, I try to be quiet and listen for God's Word to me in the passage.

Listening is not an easy task. I find myself telling God

---

4. New York: Dodd, Mead, 1962.

all that I know about the passage and how it applies to my wife or my friends or my church. But, with time, I am usually able to clear my mental screen and hear God speak out of the passage into my HEART and life.

I keep track of these "dialogues" in a journal or notebook. Some days, I fail to "show up" for my time with God. On these days I force myself to record "no entry" to note my sputtering devotion in the day-to-day crush of business and family. But, when I have time, God has time for these "talks" over his Word.

The amazing thing about meditating on Scripture is that when I do this I am no longer reading God's Word for the church, God's judgment for the world, or God's Word for anyone else. I am meditating on God's personal Word spoken directly to my HEART. Meditating on Scripture is a HEART-to-HEART encounter.

God's Word is not reserved for the theologically trained elite. His Word is for anyone at any stage of the Christian pilgrimage who will make time to listen with their HEART. Who knows more about color—a blind physicist or his housekeeper who has little formal education but has actually seen a rainbow? God has a fresh, personal word for me even when I feel too sophisticated or hurried by the press of a frantic high-tech world to listen.

CONVERSATIONS WITH GOD

Because I was raised on "sanctuary Christianity," my prayers often did not fit the real world of Monday through Saturday. I wanted to pray, but when I started to pray I would fall back into mouthing prayers that sounded like the set formulas I had always heard on Sunday morning.

I think this is a common problem. Several years ago, a Central-Texas congregation chose to open their lovely new hand-cut stone church with a renewal weekend, and invited a lay witness team to lead the weekend. After a congregational dinner on Friday, members of the visiting team were introduced, and the evening closed with prayer. Everyone prayed in little groups of four around the fellowship hall.

As the hum of praying voices faded, an elderly gentleman sprang to his feet. Ol' Charlie, a kind of "everyone's grandfather" in the church, had been in a group with two members of the lay team.

Charlie blurted out, "Hey! When these fellows pray, it sounds like they are really talking to someone!"

If I want to carry on a conversation with God—to "really talk" with him, not just rattle off pat phrases, it helps to have something specific to discuss. And here again, the Scriptures can provide a focus. Meditation over a passage of Scripture provides the subject matter through which God speaks to me. Then, once I have listened, the same passage gives me something practical to talk to God about.

That doesn't mean I am limited to talking to the content of the Scripture passage! The Scripture can provide a starting point. But I can talk to God out of practical situations at work, in my family, or in my church. I can open up my HEART to God with the strengths and weaknesses of each of the five dimensions. Out of the real situations of my HEART and life flow praise, confession of failures, requests for guidance and strength, and thanksgiving.

I need continual encouragement to follow Christ out into the hostile environment of the high-tech world. I find encouragement in honest and open conversational prayer over things that actually matter to both of us. This is prayer of the HEART.

INTERCESSION

Meditation over a passage of Scripture serves one additional function. It can bring to mind someone for whom I need to intercede in prayer. One last pass through a section of Scripture may lead me to awareness of someone with a need that only God can meet or a problem that only God can solve.

When the routine of life in the high-tech age begins to get a deadening grip on my HEART, nothing will shake its hold on me as effectively as seeing God at work in another human life. In my high-tech world with its pace and

119

pressures, people tend to become cogs in a great technological machine. I tend to see people in terms of their role or job—the secretary, the lab director, the project engineer, the technician, even the wife. Each person is labeled by the role they play, what they expect of me, and how much of my time they soak up.

But when I intercede for someone, something changes; I begin to see him or her through Christ's eyes, as a real person. As I hold this person with his or her needs and problems up to God, God is often able to get my attention to show me what my relationship with him or her should be.

Two weeks ago, a close friend in Houston called to tell me that he had noticed a pain in his jaw while jogging. So he had gone to a doctor and found he needed open-heart surgery—a quadruple bypass. I began immediately to pray for my friend's healing, for his family, and for the surgical team as they performed the operation.

As I prayed through the hours of crisis, I realized what my friend had meant to me over the years. But God also used my time of prayer to show me my serious deficiencies at being a friend and Christian brother. Through this period of intercession, I saw the reality of my friend's needs for Christ's love, healing, and forgiveness—and then discovered that my own needs were even greater!

A GOAL FOR THE SPIRITUAL DIMENSION

The six exercises I have described for developing the spiritual dimension of the HEART are simple, practical, and effective.[5] They are steps that allow Christ to become real in my life each day as I battle in the day-to-day struggle with a high-technology business.

As I launch a new business, I live daily with the emotional whiplash that comes from an entrepreneurial start-up company. Each day brings me a basketful of stress packages

---

5. The disciplines for shaping the spiritual life of a Christian have come down through the centuries in various forms. I have been helped most by Dietrich Bonhoeffer's discussion in *Life Together* (New York: Harper, 1954).

with an attached card: "You don't have time for God today." My temptation is to ignore God and spend anxious hours worrying about the competition, contacting a customer, closing a sale, finding one more technical breakthrough, the new product, cash flow, production start-up—all on my own. This high-tech age can push me into putting the spiritual dimension of my HEART to sleep.

Is there a defense, an escape from all these things that can deaden my HEART to God? My hope, and the hope of the laity in this new age, is to heed the call to keep in touch. As I master these six disciplines for the spiritual dimension, the world's grip on my HEART is broken. Each day, I must find the right combination of these exercises to open my life and world to Christ.

Only one question remains after exploring the five dimensions of the HEART: What is a biblical goal for the spiritual dimension? Jesus focused on a goal for the spiritual dimension that states the bottom line for the other four dimensions as well. On the last day of the week-long Feast of Tabernacles, Jesus stood and proclaimed, "If any one thirst, let him come to me and drink" (John 7:37).

Since this was the great Jewish feast that closed the harvest, it is not likely that anyone was still thirsty or hungry after seven days of feasting. If Jesus had spoken these words on the first day of the feast, it would appear he was about to divert the people from their religious traditions. Since it was the last day, it may indicate that he had not lost his sense of humor! But it is certain he intended to fulfill the traditions and prophecies concerning the Christ.

As Jesus continued to speak, he revealed the ultimate goal for the HEART for all who would respond to the Christ down through history. "He who believes in me, as the scripture has said, 'Out of his HEART shall flow rivers of living water.'" John adds, "Now this he said about the Spirit, which those who believe in him were to receive; for as yet the Spirit had not yet been given, because Jesus was not yet glorified" (John 7:38–39).

The age of high technology is creating a thirsty world that is cut off from spiritual reality, the source of living water. Jesus says that this living water must flow out through the five dimensions of a human HEART that is spiritually alive and growing. This is the purpose of the interior strategy of the HEART.

Psychologists and philosophers point out the spiritually stunted hearts of the high-tech age and plead for a development of spiritual values to combat growing spiritual darkness. But Jesus rises to his feet and boldly lights a flame to combat the darkness! This is spiritual reality, the life of God in the spirit of the living Christ alive in a human HEART opened to him.

The goal is not a return to the old traditions and rituals of days gone by. It is the life of God burning brightly in my will, my emotions, my ethics, my intellect, and my spiritual life as I keep in touch. A HEART of this kind is light for the spiritual darkness of the high-tech age. It is warmth to thaw the coldness of an age of high technology where HEARTs have frozen and people no longer matter.

This is the new HEART for the new age.

Part Three

MOVING OUT
IN THE
HIGH-TECH AGE

9. An Exterior Strategy

Whon I look inoido myoolf and see a growing HEART, what do I see?

Certainly not perfection! But a developing HEART does mean I have discovered God's love and forgiveness. It means I know that God, at great personal cost, accepts me as I am. In a personal encounter with Jesus Christ, I have experienced the ultimate spiritual reality—the Spirit of the living Christ in my own HEART. I have tapped the resource that eventually can overcome my weaknesses and imperfections. I know from personal experience that Christ is in the business of transforming the human HEART, and I am developing a HEART for God.

So, what's next?

Sooner or later, I will be gripped by an honest, compelling curiosity about what God has in mind for my life. I will wonder about God's expectations—and about how I can live up to those expectations in a way that reflects biblical truth while remaining responsive to the realities of the high-tech age. I will be ready to move out into the world around me.

ANSWERS TO "WHAT'S NEXT?"

But finding what God has in mind for me as I prepare to be his person in the world is not always an easy task. One reason for this difficulty is reflected in the stereotyped answers frequently given when lay men and women ask, "What's next?"

One common answer is "Not much! After all, you're only a layperson." Of course, this answer is more often implied than spoken outright. But laypeople get the message—and heed it. The trouble is that this answer is dead wrong!

Another standard reply is "Get involved in the church." (This is the answer often given by committee chairpersons in search of volunteers.) And this answer is right, of course, as far as it goes. When God becomes real in my life, he *will* lead me to participate in the life of a congregation. But involvement in the Church Gathered is only a part—perhaps even a small part—of the answer.

Still another pat answer frequently given to the layperson who has a HEART for God but who wonders what comes next is "Go full time! Attend seminary and become ordained, or at least accept a job in a Christian organization." Of course, this may be a valid call and exactly what God has in mind for me. But if it is, I move from the status of layperson to that of clergy or clericalized laity, and the role of the laity in the church is no longer a personal issue for me.

In my own life, I have struggled with these three options—doing nothing, making my church my whole ministry, and "going professional"—and I have found all three to be unacceptable for me over the long run. In this chapter, therefore, I want to examine a fourth answer to the question of "What's next?"—effective lay ministry in the high-tech world—and to consider practical suggestions for ordinary Christians who find this is what God has in mind for them.

THE PUSH TO "PROFESSIONAL CHRISTIANITY"

When I first became active in a campus ministry and discovered a congregation with an effective evangelism program, I was intrigued with the concept of "follow-up." This was defined for me as the process of teaching the basic spiritual disciplines—Bible study, prayer, and worship—to people who had recently given their lives to Christ.

But once those basics were covered, then what? It eventually struck me that the only practical "follow-up" most churches and Christian organizations could think of for laypeople like me—people who were developing our HEARTs and were ready to move out into the world—was for us to join their staff or go to the seminary. If that failed, the backup plan urged us to take on volunteer positions in the church such as Sunday school teacher or committee chairman. There were no plans or programs to support the laity or to train lay men and women in the business of being God's persons in everyday life. We were more or less abandoned with our growing HEARTs on the doorstep of the world.

Over the years, I have often been left to work out the direction of my obedience to Christ as a layman with little or no help from the congregations of which I was a member. My search for a way to be his person in the world began after I encountered Christ in a personal way on the University of Oklahoma campus. The first three years were smooth sailing in a warm, exciting campus Christian community. I led Bible studies in my fraternity house, attended discipleship classes, and got my feet wet in campus evangelism.

Then I graduated with a degree in engineering and went on to do a year of graduate study in engineering physics. And it was then that I began to feel tension in my life as I looked at the future. A number of my close friends were leaving for theological seminary or enlisting in various kinds of missionary ventures and campus ministry. I began to wonder whether I should do this, too. But I really was drawn to a high-tech career.

By Easter break, I was so torn between the lofty goal of "full-time Christian service" and the lure of high-technology industries that I retreated from my new-found Christianity. Without even realizing it, I slowly shut God out of my future. Although I still wanted him in my present—the comfortable student life there on campus—I wanted to chart the direction of my own life and to select my own occupation without God's interference.

During Easter vacation, I left Oklahoma City for job interviews in Dallas. I drove in silence for an hour, thinking. And gradually I began to realize what was happening to me. Because of my feelings of conflict over my occupational

127

decision, I was shutting the door on Christ, perhaps for the rest of my life.

I knew I didn't want that to happen. So, rolling down the interstate halfway to Texas, I reached as deeply into my life as I possibly could and prayed, "Lord, I give you my future if you'll take it. I'll do anything you want if you'll just show me what it is." As I cruised along I-35, tears rolled down my cheeks, because I knew that for the first time in my self-centered life, for an instant, I had cared more about someone or something else than I cared about myself.

Over the next few months I felt tremendous relief. The "what next" question would be answered by turning the controls of my life over to the Pilot who could fly it to its true destination. I knew that this could open up the new world of a seminary campus, mission field, or campus ministry. But I tried to remain open to whatever God had in mind for me.

CALLED TO BE A LAYPERSON?

Six months later a door finally opened for me—and it wasn't the door to the seminary! Instead, I was offered a position in the lab of a Dallas electronics company as part of a team that was developing a scientific experiment for the Mariner IV spacecraft destined for Mars.

As I prayed about the offer and the other options for study and ministry, I had a strong sense that the Dallas lab was where God wanted me to be. I had given it my best shot, so I just assumed that God knew what he was doing. I accepted the job in Dallas. If Christ was going to be real in my life, he would have to be real there in the world where God placed me. If I was to have any ministry, it would have to be lay ministry. I was shaky and timid, and at times I felt as if I had volunteered for the *professional* Christian army and been declared 4F. Still, I stepped out with the expectation that God had a special assignment for me even if I wasn't a "full-time professional."

Without realizing it, I had tapped an ancient tradition of the church. The early church recognized that Jesus Christ came for the world, not for the church, and that the church is God's provision for establishing a beachhead to reach the world. I believe the church for the high-tech age must recover that insight and build a strategy for ministry around it. When I come as a layman with a growing HEART and ask what's next, it is very reasonable and biblically correct to consider the possibility that God is calling me to lay ministry in the world where he has placed me.

Many churches, unfortunately, have a very limited concept of lay ministry as they enter the high-tech age. In order to explore God's call to lay ministry and discover what God might have in mind for us, we have to give him some room to work, even if our churches often do not. We must keep the frontiers for lay ministry open and avoid setting premature boundaries on what God may ask.

Earlier this year, I was invited by the senior minister of a large and successful church to spend half a day discussing lay ministry with his staff. When the invitation first came, the topic was described to me as "How to Get the Laity Involved in the Ministry of the Church." A few hours later, the phone rang again with the message that I had been given the wrong topic. The *correct* one was "How to Get the Church Involved in the Ministry of the Laity."

What a difference! That first topic lights up a familiar picture of efforts to get more people involved in programs down at the church. But the *second* topic opens up a new frontier. What would happen if a large affluent metropolitan congregation, with an extremely capable staff, suddenly focused its resources on enabling the congregation to be the ministers of the church out in the world where they live and work and play?

AN EXTERIOR STRATEGY

The challenge for each of us is to search out and identify our own call to lay ministry. This call to follow Jesus Christ into the world is not optional. And the task of discovering the unique shape of our individual obedience to Jesus Christ is not an easy one. I have found few healthy role models as I have struggled to identify my own ministry.

This brings us back to the issue of strategy. It should

be clear by now that I believe strategy is the key to effectiveness in lay ministry. In part 2, we examined the concept of an *interior strategy* for developing the HEART. But that is only half the picture. What must come next is an *exterior strategy* to chart the way as we explore what it means to be obedient to Christ in the high-tech world.

Such an exterior strategy should include a job description that spells out what is expected of us as the practical representatives of Jesus Christ. And it should map the territory, clearly identifying the areas in which God calls us to serve. The specifics of an exterior strategy will vary according to the individual. But there are four general areas God has designated by means of biblical mandates so we cannot miss them. The Bible makes it clear that we are to serve and minister in the arenas of work, family,[1] government, and the church.

Now, these are very general areas. And obviously, these four arenas of life are not reserved exclusively for Christians. I have sometimes wondered if, in specifying these four arenas, the biblical writers were simply observing the general activities that were already going on around them. But the Bible indicates that the very reasons these activities were going on in the first place is that God had mandated them for *all* people.

THE SECULAR-SACRED SPLIT

From a biblical perspective, then, all people in the world are meant to function in these four basic arenas of life. Unfortunately, the tendency is for Christians and non-Christians alike to group work, family, and government together as "secular," while setting the church aside as "sacred."

But there are some serious problems with this secular-

---

1. This could also be called "the arena of marriage" and in the biblical sense still be inclusive of the family. Bonhoeffer uses the term "marriage" instead of "family," but describes marriage as the place where children are produced and educated to be obedient to Jesus Christ by parents who are representatives of God to the child (see footnote 2). Martin Luther spoke of three primary orders that God the Creator provided: the family, the state, and the church. The economic order that deals with daily work was grouped with the family; in my opinion, however, that is not an adequate (or biblical) concept for today's world.

sacred division. First and foremost, it is a nonbiblical view; it simply is not at all what God had in mind. The second problem is that it tends to cut God out of the three "secular" arenas (work, family, and government) and to allow the power of sin unrestrained freedom to devastate and wreck lives. A third problem is the tendency to isolate the church from the rest of human life. This isolation can transform the church from a source of strength and renewal into a theater of irrelevant ritual.

Given that these four arenas of life should not be split into sacred or secular, what is the difference between lay ministry carried out in these areas and day-to-day life in these four arenas as lived by everyone else? What makes the call to each of these four arenas a divine mandate? They become divine when Jesus Christ becomes real for us in the very center of each of the four arenas. German theologian and pastor Dietrich Bonhoeffer put it this way:

> It is God's will that there shall be labor, marriage, government and church in the world; and it is His will that all these, each in its own way, shall be through Christ, directed towards Christ, and in Christ. This means that there can be no retreating from a "secular" into a "spiritual" sphere. There can be only the practice, the learning, of the Christian life under these four mandates of God. These mandates are, indeed, divine only by virtue of their original and final relation to Christ.[2]

The four divine mandates take on special significance for those of us who set out with Christ to develop the HEART. When we set foot in each arena, we are called to responsible obedience to Jesus Christ in that particular part of his world. When we step into each arena, we must ask what it means to be Christ's person in that place.

The personal strategy of each lay man and woman must include being Christ's person in work, family, government, and the church. This is not an easy call to obey, but it is a very difficult call to avoid. In the following chapters of

2. *Ethics* (New York: Macmillan, 1965), p. 207.

part three, these four arenas will be examined from a lay perspective. When we open each arena of our lives to Jesus Christ, God removes the secular/spiritual labels and establishes his claim on the territory.

THE NEED FOR BALANCE

These four arenas are definite assignments for the laity. They cannot be ignored or reprioritized, but must be held in balance. When this balance is not maintained, the result is what I call "mission with omission." For example, it is possible for me to set out to save the world and, in the process, to neglect my family. Or I can concentrate exclusively on my family life while ignoring the needy world outside the four walls of the home. A familiar example I see here in Dallas is that of the business executive or entrepreneur who goes all-out in the work arena at the expense of family and church. And behind the familiar reliance on "big government" to care for people who apparently cannot care for themselves may lie an unbalanced avoidance of tasks that should be undertaken by the private sector under the leadership of lay men and women.

As I understand it, an external strategy must involve a commitment to understand, master, and excel at these four divinely mandated arenas of work, family, government, and church. If I am to take this responsibility seriously as a follower of Jesus Christ, I need a developing HEART for the task. When I step into any of the four arenas, my life and relationship with Jesus Christ must focus on that arena. I have not developed my HEART in union with Christ to retreat to a quiet cabin on a mountain lake to contemplate.

The process of developing the HEART and then moving out into the world is for ordinary Christians in the ordinary situations of life. Christ becomes real in these four arenas of life as our obedience to him becomes real. In the words of Thomas Merton, "It is in the ordinary duties and labors of life that the Christian can and should develop a spiritual union with God."[3] I am called by God and assigned to lay

---

3. *Life and Holiness* (Garden City, NY: Image Books, 1964), p. 9.

ministry in the areas of my work, my family, my government, and the church.

THE QUESTION OF THE CALL

A common roadblock for ordinary Christians as they try to respond to Christ's call to ministry is the tendency of the Christian community not to recognize service and work in the world as a Christian calling. This goes back to the attitude that only "professional" Christian service counts. Where this attitude prevails, lay men and women are never directly challenged to examine their obedience to Jesus Christ in the areas of work, family, and government.

I keep a clipping from a local congregational newspaper that reveals this prevailing mindset in an embarrassing way:

> _____, an attorney, has been a member of _____ church for twelve years. He interrupted his membership and his legal career for nearly a year to devote himself to Christian service.

The article goes on to say that before taking his leave of absence, this attorney had taught Sunday school, been chairman of the board of deacons, and had been an elder.

This human interest blurb leaves the impression that God finally called this man to something _important_—some full-time Christian service that clearly outranked serving the needs of his clients as a lawyer or the needs of the congregation as a teacher, deacon, or elder. (As a matter of fact, he left his law practice to cook at a Christian conference center.)

As preparation for the high-tech age, I believe the church must finally straighten out its confused concept of vocation, which literally means "calling." In the period of church history prior to Martin Luther, the church taught that only priests, nuns, and monks had vocations; everyone else in the church simply had jobs. The unfortunate assumption was that God only "called" religious professionals.

When the word _vocation_ was finally applied to the laity, it was done so by the business world, not the church. Luther and Calvin made progress on redefining _vocation_ for the laity, but the secular world beat them to it.

Even today, when people speak of a vocation or of "finding their calling," they mean that they have selected their career or profession. But who has called them? No one, really. *Vocation* is actually an exclusively Christian concept because it is God who calls us in Jesus Christ to our tasks in the world and the church.

When I filter my call from God through a growing HEART, I hear above everything else a call to responsible personal obedience to Jesus Christ. But I also hear a call to a place of ministry in the church, the Body of Christ. I am called to minister in the church—to build up and strengthen the Body of Christ. I am called to daily work in my job or occupation from which I derive my livelihood. (This includes work inside the home, which may not draw a paycheck but is nonetheless daily work!) God may call me to serve in my community or nation or even the world without pay. Life is complex and, since God calls me, he must guide me in balancing my life in these four arenas.

When the four arenas are laid out side by side, the key difference between clergy and laity becomes clear. The clergy's call to the church and call to an occupation are one and the same—just as a homemaker's call to work and to the family are in the same area. But the laity have one call to a job or occupation, by which they support themselves, and an equally serious call to the church, which does not involve earning a living.

All of these calls are honorable. But unfortunately, many people consciously or unconsciously hold to the primitive concept that the only valid "call" from God is to "full-time" Christian service. I believe it is time for clergy and laity alike to recognize that God calls the laity both to the church and to an occupation. I believe the church must develop a greater sensitivity to the tremendous tension experienced by ordinary lay men and women who have a HEART for God and who struggle to balance these two arenas of life.

If there is a real biblical role model and hero for the laity in the high-tech age, it is Paul. Paul's occupation was that of tentmaker, which is where he "drew his paycheck." But his vocation in the church was that of being the Apostle to the Gentiles, but he wasn't paid a dime (or denari) for it. (An ironic twist is that Paul is also one of the best-selling authors in the history of the world, but never received a royalty check.)

A CALL TO CHRISTIAN LEADERSHIP

I believe the critical issue for the church in the high-tech age is leadership. Ordinary Christians with a developing HEART for God must have competent leaders and become competent leaders to the limit of their God-given gifts and abilities. It is naive to assume that following Christ in any of the four arenas of life will not pose a major leadership challenge.

But when I use the term "leadership," I am using it in a slightly different sense from the way it is often used. For I do not believe that the most important leadership for the church in the high-tech age will come from the kind of great and gifted charismatic leaders whom everyone can admire but with whom no one can identify. Instead, the church will be motivated by low-profile leaders whose main qualification will be that they have made progress in getting their own acts together while helping fellow strugglers.

If I am developing resources of the HEART and I am open and vulnerable as I struggle with the real issues of life in my work, family, and church, people will wander up to see how I do it. Soon, they will want to get in on something that works. And before I know it, I will be a leader—whether the world recognizes it or not.

A critical need of the church for the high-tech age will be this kind of leader—the ordinary person whose life has been touched by Jesus Christ, whose HEART is growing and developing, and who takes obedience to Jesus Christ very seriously in the arenas of work, family, government, and church. I call such a person an "e-Leader" (lowercase e), after the "elders" in the first-century church. I believe this leadership style must be affirmed, recognized, and adopted as a goal for ordinary Christians in a high-tech world.

The model for a church which operates successfully with e-Leaders is the church that flourished in the first three hundred years after the death of Christ. During this period, there were no clergy, no seminaries, and no church buildings. The church was in the hands of people who were not religious professionals—the elders who developed the pattern of the e-Leader.

Imagine a church with no gothic buildings, no senior ministers or priests preaching, no visiting theology professors lecturing! In such a situation, what would church members do with themselves? Mark Gibbs and T. Ralph Winter suggest an answer for the Christians who found themselves in this situation during the church's first three-hundred-year period. They converted the Roman Empire![4]

In our time, however, the Church Gathered is, with few exceptions, organized in the form of an institution, and therefore it has a need for people to run the institution. These, too, are leaders—but they fulfill a different role in the church. I call leaders of the organized, institutional church E-Leaders (capital *E*).

I use these unusual (some have said *"oddball"*) terms for several reasons. First and foremost, they emphasize the need for leadership as lay men and women respond to the call to follow Christ in the high-tech world. They also emphasize the difficulty that serious lay leaders have in balancing their commitments to serve both in the Church Gathered and the Church Scattered. Finally, using the terms "e-Leader" and "E-Leader" permits me to examine general leadership needs and styles without running aground on specific organizational structures and titles used in various denominations.

In the chapters to come, I will be looking at each of the four arenas in which Christians are called to participate—work, family, government, and church. But because I feel leadership is so important for the church in the high-tech age, I have divided discussion of the arena of the church into two different chapters—one on the Church Scattered

---

4. *God's Frozen People* (Philadelphia: Westminster, 1964).

and one on the Church Gathered—on the basis of this issue.

The term "Church Scattered," if you remember, refers to the people of the church out in the world of their daily lives, Monday through Saturday. This seems to be the best place to explore the e-Leader's style, because here the structure of the institutional church is simply not an issue. The e-Leader's role can be studied without rewriting the history of the various denominations that omit elders from their organizational charts.

In a later chapter, I look at the church as the Church Gathered—the people of God who have come together in tho buildings on a church campus for worship, study, and ministry. In that chapter, I will be discussing the role of the organizational E-Leader.

PORTRAIT OF A LEADER

I am fortunate to have had the opportunity of observing a close friend of mine develop e-Leader characteristics as he ministered to his friends and fellow members of a Texas congregation. Don managed his own business, and as sometimes happens, he also served on the official board of his congregation (as an E-Leader).

A clue to Don's effectiveness came the year that his church decided to take nominations for the office of elder (member of the governing board) by asking the members of the congregation to write on a card the name of the person in the congregation who had helped them the most personally. Don led the poll. God had used him in simple, nonspectacular ways to serve and minister to his friends and associates.

But an even more dramatic testimony to Don's influence occurred years after Don had moved to another city. One winter, a group from his former church was on their annual retreat—an event Don had helped start years earlier. As the retreat began, each person shared why he or she was there. As they went around the circle, they discovered that many of the stories had a common thread. Don was the reason they were on the journey with Jesus Christ.

Don's phone rang that dreary February night. Someone

137

was calling from the retreat center. Then there was another caller, then another. One by one, a dozen people left that sharing circle to come to the phone and say, "You are the reason I'm here. Thank you!"

Out of Don's struggle to balance his direct ministry to individuals (e-Leader) with congregational oversight (E-Leader) came the results—changed lives. Most of us will never get a call like the one he received. But if each of us is faithful to follow the call of Christ into the world where he puts us, some day, when we are together in person with the Lord Jesus Christ, our fellow workers, neighbors, church members, friends, and family can say, "You're the reason I'm here. Thank you."

Christ's call to follow him in the high-tech age is unique and personal. Each of us has specific tasks we can do better than anyone else. But there are some basic principles that apply to all of us as we go about the task of being God's people in the high-tech age. In the chapters to come, I want to look at some specific ideas for developing a personal exterior strategy for the arenas of church (both the Church Scattered and the Church Gathered), daily work, family, and government.

10. The Arena of the Church (Scattered)

The Church Scattered is the church between Sundays. When the last hymn has been sung and the benediction pronounced, I walk out the doors of the sanctuary into the world of the Church Scattered. What happens to the lay men and women who step out into the high-tech age for six days depends on their attitudes and expectations. For those who check their Christian minds at the door when they leave the church, nothing will happen. For those who develop a personal exterior strategy for life and ministry in the Church Scattered, life becomes very, very interesting.

I have found lay ministry in the arena of the Church Scattered to be difficult, demanding, and often lonely. The world is a tough place to serve Jesus Christ in the high-tech age or any other age.

The local congregation may not be much help, especially if you are in a "caretaker" congregation whose idea of lay ministry is having a layperson pass the offering plates. But support may also be scarce in congregations that claim to believe in lay ministry, because so many congregations think of lay ministry only in terms of activities that are performed in church buildings or in programs officially sponsored by the congregation.

Such introverted thinking about lay ministry tempts me to add to the list of "Greatest Lies in the World." (Lie #1 is, "The check is in the mail." Lie #2 is, "I'll still love you in the morning." Lie #3: "I am from the government and I am here to help you.") I would propose as Lie #4: "We are on the staff of the church and we want to support you in your lay ministry."

139

Now, I don't mean to say that church staffs and congregations are deliberately perpetrating falsehoods. But my experience has been that few laypersons ever get a visit from the clergy in their world of work and ministry. When clergy do come to discuss "lay ministry," they usually mean they need help with some program or project at the church. The plans have been laid by the staff in midweek meetings, and the laity are expected to support the project with time and money under the heading "lay ministry."

GOD'S PEOPLE IN THE WORLD

As I work to define my personal strategy for the Church Scattered, I am continually forced to seek an enlarged and sharper vision of what we are about as God's people in the world. The summer before my senior year at the university, I was accepted in the Summer CO-OP Program of Geophysical Service, Inc.—at that time, the world's largest petroleum exploration company. From my first contact with the company, the thing that captured my imagination was the corporate motto: "The world is your office when you explore for oil with GSI."

The time has come when ordinary Christians assigned by Christ to the Church Scattered also need a corporate motto: "The world is your office when you follow Jesus Christ!" This motto is a reminder that, if God can be real in the church, he can be real in the world between Sundays. The important thing is that we give God the freedom to show us new frontiers of lay ministry once we step off the church grounds.

The parallel between lay ministry and oil exploration continues a little farther. At the beginning of the Summer CO-OP Program, students were wined and dined in Dallas for a week and treated to technical lectures by industry leaders. We were fired up! But when we were given our summer assignments on the last afternoon of that orientation week, I began to wonder what we had gotten into. They told the fellow next to me to go to Greybull, Wyoming, and ask the people at the Mobil Station if they knew where the GSI crew had gone!

140

Actually, I wasn't too worried, because I knew I was going to the Rio Grande Valley and wouldn't even have to leave Texas. But by evening my orders had changed, and the next day I was making the drive into the Mississippi Delta to join a crew working there. I had a tight knot in the pit of my stomach because I had been assigned to work in a swamp where no boats or trucks could go. I lost twenty pounds in two weeks from packing equipment in Turtle Bayou. I found out that the previous two Summer CO-OP students on this crew had walked off the job and were never heard from again.

STEPPING OUT INTO "THE SWAMP"

My first venture into lay ministry felt a lot like Turtle Bayou. When the time finally came for me to leave the University of Oklahoma campus for the electronics business in Dallas, I was fired up and convinced that this was what God wanted me to do. But a few weeks later I hit the spiritual swamp, and I knew I was on my own. If I had gone to seminary, I would have received graduate training and then started my ministry "under care" of a church. If I had signed up for a campus ministry, I would have headed directly to the national headquarters for a cram course in student evangelism, followed by a field training assignment. But in the Church Scattered, where I felt I had been called, it was sink or swim.

My first step was to find someone who knew what he was doing and get with him. I had met a local oil company executive named Keith Miller, who lived near the campus in Norman, Oklahoma. I often heard this man teach Sunday school and speak about his faith. I knew that he had been president of my social fraternity a few years before I came to the university and had tried the road I was headed down both with and without Christ. So I called Keith and told him that I'd like to talk to him about being a Christian in my new job.

Keith invited me over and listened patiently as I explained where I thought God was sending me. Finally, I laid out my main concern. What do I do to share my faith in Christ

141

when I get to Texas Instruments? Keith replied very casually, "Don't worry. When people find out you are a Christian, they will come to you."

When I got to my job, I tried to make it obvious that I was a Christian. I had Christian books and often a Bible piled on my desk a good part of the time, because I love to read. I was never shy about discussing my activities in the singles' group at a local Presbyterian church. When Christmas came, I even passed out some rather tasteful literature on becoming a Christian. Two years passed. No one came to me.

I began to remember and question Miller's advice. The more I thought about it, the more convinced I became that his basic idea was correct. The problem was, no one seemed to have found out I was a Christian! That was why no one came to me.

Years later, I reminded Keith of his advice and added, with a slight twist of the knife, "I tried it for two years and no one came." He had the look of a man who was watching a garbage truck back over his new car.

Keith cringed and shook his head: "Oh no, Slocum! What I meant was, people would experience God's love and concern coming through you and be drawn to you."

He was off the hook because by then I knew what he had meant. I know *now*. But I had to learn the lesson.

TAKING TO THE SLOPES

There have been many, many lessons that I have had to learn and am still learning. For me, learning lay ministry has been a lot like learning to ski. It was a matter of working hard at doing unnatural things in a strange environment!

Years ago, when I was working in Seattle, I met an engineer I'd gone to school with in Oklahoma. We hit it off, and we thought it would be fun to do things together. The only trouble was we couldn't decide what to do.

He said, "Let's go hunting." I said, "That is how I lost my ear." I said, "Let's play handball." He said, "That is

142

how I lost my eye." Finally, we compromised on a ski trip to Mt. Hood in Oregon. (I promise that this will be the last mountain story!)

I didn't have any idea what I was doing. That weekend, I had to make do with poorly fitting rental equipment and a place to sleep on the floor of a room at Timberline Lodge.

A nurse who had come with us suggested that I ride up the chair lift with her. The view was spectacular, but halfway up the mountain I realized I'd never been on a chair lift before in my life! Just as we reached the exit ramp, something grabbed the tips of my skis and nearly pulled me out of the chair. The instant I recovered from snagging my ski tip, I looked down and saw that the ramp was totally blocked by a lady in red who had fallen in a lifeless heap. I froze as the ground rapidly receded, and for a split second, I thought the chairs were turning upside down before heading back down the mountain. So I jumped and made a perfect Nordic landing—directly on top of the red-clad lady who was trying to get up.

Finally, I got untangled from the pileup and wobbled out onto the slope that rolled down the mountain for a mile. And I realized I was looking at a mile of solid ice!

My only ski maneuver was a shaky snowplow turn, which I soon found is absolutely worthless on ice. So at this point I invented the Slocum Ski Method. I started near the edge of the run and traversed the slope, crashing into the trees and bushes on the opposite side. Then I picked myself up and did it again, and again, for two fun-packed hours, because I didn't know how to turn!

This method of controlled crashes, which I call "Learning by Bumping into Things," is, unfortunately, the same one I used to learn lay ministry. I would start out in the world with someone else's ill-fitting equipment and with inadequate training and would just keep going until I ended up in a pileup after smashing into someone. When I finally got to the place where the action was supposed to be, the little that I *did* know how to do often didn't work. So I crashed, over and over, until I began to think that if I had any sense I would have stayed in the lodge. After all, the

Christian Army is still the only army that gives medals for staying in the barracks.

Somehow, despite the trauma, I kept working at lay ministry and got a little smarter. When Linda and I got married, we spent a Christmas honeymoon in Crested Butte, a picturesque mining town in Colorado with a fantastic ski lodge. I had not had a ski lesson since Mt. Hood, and, at any rate, skiing was not our top priority at that period of time. But we found a ski instructor who had learned his trade as an army ski trooper, and the ski bug bit harder than the love bug. Ten consecutive lessons later, we were cruising down from the top of the mountain with a fair degree of style and safety. And I found that skiing was a lot more fun with a committed partner and a great instructor.

This was also true of the next section of my personal strategy for the arena of the Church Scattered. If I had continued to try lay ministry alone and ill-prepared, I would eventually either have given up or continued making a fool of myself on a regular basis. But the call to follow Christ in the world does not disappear just because we ignore the call or follow him badly! We are responsible for doing what we can to get better—and this means finding partners who will commit to the mission, so we can support and encourage each other. We must find knowledgeable instructors who can help us identify our mission and then guide and equip us as we develop our skills.

In my own experience God has been faithful to guide me to places of encouragement and equipping for lay ministry. When I have begun to pray and search, he has raised up partners and instructors. I have been blessed over the years with congregations that were not afraid of lay ministry—although I have also had contact with many other congregations that seemed to have no idea what to do with the laity. God seems to have moved me from one oasis in the desert to the next. Much encouragement has come from beyond the congregation, from individuals and parachurch organizations with a vision of an empowered, equipped laity serving as Christ's body in the world.

A COMMITMENT TO BEING THE CHURCH SCATTERED

I often wonder why the institutional church has such a dim vision and weak commitment to lay ministry in the Church Scattered. Throughout this century, most major denominations have taken a "fresh look" at the subject of lay ministry every five or ten years. But after a conference or two, it is usually put back in its case and returned to the shelf for another five or ten years. My best explanation is loss of memory. The institutional church has lost its collective memory of what the world was like when each follower of Jesus Christ considered the world to be his or her office for ministry, work, and service for Jesus Christ.

There was a time when the Church Scattered took this mission seriously. During the first three hundred years of the church, when there were no church buildings, no seminaries, and no professional clergy, the church had little institutional form. It did have an internal shape and structure provided by lay leaders, the "elders" that fit the e-Leader pattern I described in chapter 9. And ordinary Christians modeled their roles in the Church Scattered after what they saw the elders doing.

An elder in Rome who was a leather worker lived above his shop on a street with other leather workers and shoemakers. He did not have cross-town bus service to carry him out of his neighborhood to church. His ministry was directed toward his family, his friends, his customers, and even his co-workers and competitors up and down his street and alley. The body of Christ came alive on the spot because of the ministry and lives of such Christians.

MAKING OF AN e-LEADER

The first-century elder was an extremely effective e-Leader in the absence of paid clergy and church professionals. But elder selection and training was a tremendous gamble. An apostle such as Paul would arrive in a particular town, preach that Jesus Christ had risen from the dead, round up all the Jews and Gentiles who would respond to his message, and teach them a cram course on "The Way" before he left town. Then would come time for Paul to move on, and there was no bishop, no presbytery, no seminary to send a replacement. They couldn't even raid the church in the next town for a pastor!

The apostle had no choice. He had to put in charge those local people who, in his opinion, had the best chance of keeping the church going. Paul had to risk letting those amateurs run the church into the ground.

From where we sit today in the institutional church, it is hard to picture the inexperienced, wild, and woolly bunch of converts Paul and the other apostles had on their nomination lists for leadership in the early churches. (The lists of what *not* to choose gives us an idea of what there was to choose from!) Yet, the future of each local congregation was gambled on the hope that God could use these men to keep the Christian enterprise afloat.

Some idea of what Peter and Paul experienced as they selected these leaders can be extracted from their advice on the subject. (The texts are found in Paul's first letter to Timothy, 3:1–7, and Peter's first letter, 5:1–4.) Let me paraphrase what these two apostles said *not* to look for: Do *not* select someone who stays drunk, gets drunk and picks fights, loves to start arguments, or would use the church to make a dollar. Skip the men who have more than one wife. Pass over the green recruits who tend to get conceited, as well as anyone who turns into a bossy tyrant when he gets control. You do not need anyone with a bad reputation in the community who could give the church a bad name by being caught in a scandal or shady business deal.

So . . . scratch a few names. But what do we look for? The letters of Peter and Paul spell out guidelines for an e-Leader that are so practical and effective that I suggest each lay man and woman adopt them as goals for both leadership and ministry: The e-Leader must be:

- a good, practical teacher
- a good manager of his (or her) household and children

146

- willing to care for other people
- a courteous, hospitable model of the faith.

These requirements are startling in their simplicity. What about academic background and theological training? What about restrictions based on social or financial standing? What about a charismatic, attractive personality? What about "people skills" and the ability to manage other people? Peter and Paul make no mention of any of these things. What counts according to these two apostles is an active faith, a sound life, and the faithful discharge of duties in the church and community.

The e-Leader based on the early-church model is a servant of a few rather than a leader of the masses. God must have anticipated that highly visible leaders would be required to oversee the institutional church's buildings, schools, programs, and paid staff, and over the centuries he has called such leaders. But he has always left the back door open to anyone—lay or clergy—who would take seriously the call to be a servant in the role of an e-Leader.

In the high-tech age, the offices of priest, pastor, bishop, pope, and senior minister will not go away—and I am not saying that they should. But I believe that each layperson must develop a personal strategy based on the knowledge that the future of the church will rest with the e-Leaders, the faithful servants, just as it did during the church's first three centuries—and those leaders are just as likely to be found among the laity as they are to be religious professionals or clergy.

GOALS FOR e-LEADERS

Even as a scientist with an introverted personality and highly technical special interests, I can hear Christ calling me to certain leadership goals each day (although sometimes he has to shout). One of these goals is to *become a teacher* of the disciplines of a life committed to Jesus Christ. This is an intensely personal task which involves explaining clearly how my faith works for me. I may be called to teach one-on-one, lead a group, or conduct a class. And I must also model a practical walk with Christ for the people who do their "on-the-job" leadership training with me. Being a teacher doesn't mean I have to know everything, however. In fact, when I look at the teachers and mentors in my own life, I find I don't rate them on total knowledge at all. The high scores go to those who got across to me exactly how their faith worked in such a practical way that I could understand and use it myself.

Care of my marriage and family are also priority goals for me as an e-Leader and are targeted as a divine mandate. But the act of giving top priority to marriage and family is a strange and countercultural idea in this high-tech world. Families are fractured by divorce, physical and sexual abuse, alcohol and chemical dependency, and they are often held together only by the unraveling threads of damaged relationships. And this is true of many church families as well as those outside the church. In fact, the church has an unenviable record of letting leaders "burn out" in the service of the church while their families and marriages fall apart from neglect. Whatever the sorry state of families in the high-tech age, and whatever family and marriage conditions that have come to be tolerated as "normal," e-Leaders must face the call to serve their families as a direct act of obedience to Jesus Christ.

A final characteristic of an e-Leader is the *ability and willingness to accept responsibility for people and to care for them as a minister of Jesus Christ.* In the original biblical context, this could not have meant just preaching to the masses or overseeing the programs and activities of the church the way it's often done today by church boards and professional staffs. The task was one-on-one; the e-Leader actually reached out and touched the lives of the people under his care. We can learn to do the same thing if we simply are available to God.

The ministry modeled on the e-Leader pattern is not a ministry to which we are appointed. It is a ministry of authority that comes from being a loving servant to a few people. All we may have to show for it is the knowledge that we have been servants of Jesus Christ, of our families, and of the handful of people God has given each of us to care for, love, teach, and share life with. It is very likely that the world, or even the church, may never notice. But the future of the church in the high-tech age rests with the men and women who have the HEART to provide this kind of leadership.

THE MISSION OF THE CHURCH SCATTERED

I am convinced that if the church is to be effective in the high-tech age, it must recover this mission of the Church Scattered. When I am called to follow Christ, I may have to ask what it means to be his person in a corporation as well as in a congregation, in a neighborhood park as well as on the church grounds. I must understand what role Christ calls me to play in the church outside the sanctuary, and to balance that role with my occupation and my personal relationship with Christ.

Here again, Paul is a helpful model. The apostle Paul called himself a bond slave of Jesus Christ; no call in his life was higher than the call to a personal relationship with his Lord. But Paul also had an occupation. He worked as a tentmaker, and this is how he made his living and how he met two of his closest friends, Priscilla and Aquila. The role Paul was called to fill as part of the Church Scattered— the body of Christ beyond the temple gates—was that of Apostle to the Gentiles. These three calls he held in balance throughout his ministry.

As a layman in the Church Scattered today, I must build my life around the fact that God will use me to bring the body of Christ to life in the world. When Jesus was on earth in a physical body, he did his Father's will by the power of the Holy Spirit. Today, the Spirit is in residence in the many dimensions of my HEART, and I have been given spiritual gifts to serve the body of Christ. My strategy for lay ministry must reflect this reality. The challenge for me as a leader in the Church Scattered is seeing Christ come alive and touch lives in the corner of the world where God places me. I must find someone or some need and respond in obedience to Jesus Christ.

149

SEEING IT WORK

Despite my "two-year drought" when I first came to Texas Instruments, I've discovered what it's like when God uses me in the world where I live and work. Keith Miller was right. People do come to you when they see Christ at work in your life.

After graduate school, I returned to TI to direct new product development in a specialized area of submarine detection. After a staff meeting one morning, I grabbed a cup of coffee with the manufacturing manager of our department. It was late fall, and as we walked down to his office, we were discussing skiing plans for the winter and the rising cost of skiing.

Jim dropped into his desk chair and said, "I've got worse problems than that. Joan and I separated last night."

I didn't even know Jim was married! We just worked in the same department and talked skiing occasionally at coffee break. But I shut the door and sat down while Jim poured out a rather confusing story of a messed-up marriage. He said the only advice he had gotten so far was some tips from his buddies at the local yacht club about how to keep from losing everything in a divorce.

I got up my courage and finally said, "Jim, if you and Joan want to put this marriage back together, I believe there are spiritual and technical resources available to help you do it." Then, I sat there in an awkward silence, wondering if Jim thought I was some kind of fool.

He finally leaned forward and looked me in the eye. "I'm not a religious person. But last night I got down on my knees and said, 'God, if you are out there and care, I could sure use some help.' "

The help for Jim and Joan took an interesting path. The first stop was a Christian marriage counselor who specialized in crisis intervention. Joan was found to be experiencing depression that had physical causes and could be treated with medication. They continued with weekly counseling sessions. And then they started getting up early on Sunday morning, after late nights at the yacht club, to attend a couples' Sunday school class I was teaching.

After a month or so, Jim and Joan decided to join a small group that was starting in the home of a sales executive and his wife. The first night, the leader of the group threw out as an opening question, "What does commitment mean to you?"

Jim quickly answered, "Commitment is like when you decide to get married, or when you decide not to get a divorce like Joan and I did two weeks ago."

The third week, the group discussed commitment to Jesus Christ. And the next morning Jim cornered me at work. He wanted to know exactly what I thought commitment to Christ meant. I suggested that we go to lunch the following week, and I said I would tell him my story of my own encounter with Christ and what it meant in my life. Jim wanted to know why we couldn't have lunch *that day*. So that day over lunch I told Jim my story.

On the way back to the plant, I asked Jim if what I had said made sense to him. He said it did. I asked Jim if there was any reason why he couldn't commit his life to Christ right at that moment. He said he couldn't. And he had some surprisingly good reasons, because his life was a complicated mess.

As we walked across the parking lot of the plant and he told me some more about his background, I had an insight about what the core of Jim's problem might be. I said, "Jim, you seem to be carrying a big bag of crap over your shoulder that contains all the sins you've ever committed. You act like the only way you can get all this straightened out with God is to go forward in some little church [like the one in which he grew up], confess everything you've ever done wrong, and never sin again as long as you live."

Jim sheepishly admitted that I might be pretty close. I asked him, "If you can do all that, what do you need Christ for?"

That night, Jim and Joan got on their knees together and committed their lives and their marriage to Jesus Christ.

The morning Jim first talked to me about his marriage, I had gotten up early to read from Sam Shoemaker's *With*

151

the Holy Spirit and with Fire.[1] I had picked out a prayer and used it that morning: "Lord, keep me in the stream of the Spirit this day." I saw my prayer answered. Because of my availability and his power, God had let me see the miracle of Christ bringing new life through me as part of the Church Scattered in the high-tech world.

1. Waco, TX: Word Books, 1960.

11. The Arena of Work

Of the four arenas in which lay men and women are called to serve, perhaps the least understood by the church today is the arena of daily work in the world. Yet this is the arena in which we, the laity, spend the largest proportion of our time in the high-tech age.

During my graduate-school days at the University of Texas, I read *The Christian in Business,* by John E. Mitchell, Jr.[1] One day a colleague of mine, a very bright physics student, spotted the book on my desk and offhandedly remarked, "I guess if you are a Christian in business, you can't make a profit." My agnostic friend at least had sensed that being a Christian should make some kind of difference in the work arena, but this wasn't it. I fired back impatiently, "No, Mike! If you don't make a profit, you are not a Christian in business; you are a Christian who just went out of business."

But what *does* it mean to follow Jesus Christ into the work arena? The ethical and moral issues are so complex as we enter the high-tech age that it is hard even to find a basic starting point from which to examine the world of work. But it is nevertheless important for each of us—whether it be in a corporation, school, trade, industry, the home, or a profession—to make an effort to discover what it means to be the people of God in the workplace where Christ calls us.

---

1. Westwood, NJ: Revell, 1962.

SOME GUIDELINES FOR HEARTS IN THE WORKPLACE

A number of years ago, I was preparing to teach an informal seminar on "developing the HEART" to a group of Texas Instruments employees and their spouses. I contacted Dr. Michael Maccoby, the psychologist, whose writings had first drawn my attention to the problem of underdeveloped HEARTs in high-technology workers.[2] Maccoby seemed pleased that someone was making an effort to work on the problem, so we made plans to meet during my next visit to Washington, D.C.

As I drove through the parklike woods to Dr. Maccoby's home, I experienced a mild anxiety attack, wondering if this "noted authority" on the HEART could scan me with X-ray vision and somehow grade me on the development of my own HEART. But my fears quickly melted as we began a relaxed conversation that ranged from the health problems of hard-driving Texas Instruments managers to the development level of President Jimmy Carter's HEART. (Carter was in office at the time.)

Then Maccoby quite unintentionally struck a nerve with a casual question: "What difference has development of your HEART made in your own work?"

My mind went blank. I kicked myself for not anticipating that this question would come up and preparing my answer. I fumbled around and came up with something about helping people keep from becoming underemployed in a large corporation. The truth was that in some areas it had not made any difference, and in some areas it *had* made a difference. But I was not prepared to tell my story because I found it difficult to focus on the HEART in the context of my daily work. This conversation with Dr. Maccoby made me more keenly aware of the key issue for those of us who would follow Jesus Christ into the work arena of the high-tech age: the conscious, intentional impact the development of the HEART has on daily work.

The arena of daily work is the last frontier of the HEART

------

2. See chapter 3.

and most resistant to the positive influence of a developed HEART. And because so many in the church still refuse truly to accept work in the world as a valid Christian calling, many lay men and women are never confronted with the need to discover the shape of their obedience to Christ in their work and labor.

During my working career, I have been employed in my parents' business, by two major U.S. corporations, and by two large universities. In the last few years, I have worked in my own consulting and manufacturing business. I must honestly state that over the years I have received very little help from any congregation of which I have been a member as I have tried to discover what it means to be Christ's person in my daily work. And I can't understand this willingness to ignore the fact that God is actually concerned about how his people function in the work arena.

This concern of God's is laced through both the Old and New Testaments. Even though the work culture of biblical times was radically different from that of the high-tech age, it is nevertheless possible to draw from these rich resources to pull together a set of guidelines for daily work that are still practical and relevant today. These guidelines outline the process by which a growing HEART can influence our jobs, professions, occupations, or careers. (My own experience involves "going to work" at an office or laboratory and receiving monetary compensation, and the terms I use in this chapter reflect that. But I believe these biblical guidelines for daily work also apply to homemakers, those in volunteer service, and others whose daily work follows a different pattern.)

A DIVINE MANDATE AND A TOOL OF GOD

The first guideline refers back to the fact that work is a divine mandate—decreed by God to be an important part of our lives. In the words of the Psalmist: "Man goes forth to his work and to his labor until the evening" (Ps. 104:23). Because work originated with God, it follows that *we are to look at work as something to which God calls us and*

155

as something he can use to give divine order to our lives.

When we look at work in this light, certain other issues become clear. For instance, we begin to see that the *where* and the *why* of our daily work must come from obedience to Christ. Certain occupations, such as those that are harmful to individuals or the community, will become unacceptable to us. When we open our work lives to Christ, God's guidance and timing can take us from unhealthy work arenas to healthy ones.

The *how* of daily work is also Christ's concern. There are styles of work that are unacceptable to God. Thomas Merton hit the "style of work" issue head-on in his book, *Life and Holiness,* when he wrote,

> Work in a normal, healthy human context, work with a sane and moderate human measure, integrated in a productive social milieu, is by itself capable of contributing much to the spiritual life. But work that is disordered, irrational, unproductive, dominated by the exhausting frenzies and wastefulness of a worldwide struggle for power and wealth, is not necessarily going to make a valid contribution to the spiritual lives of all those engaged in it. Hence it is important to consider the nature of work and its place in the Christian Life.[3]

When I stop and look at the irrational, unproductive, and exhausting frenzies of my own work life, I can't help wondering where all of these confusing activities come from. It is clear that I need the divine order God can give to my work life. I mean to serve God in the work arena, but all too often my life in the workplace resembles Merton's description of life in the Cistercian order at Gethsemani Monastery, where he lived:

> The Cistercian life is energetic. There are tides of vitality running through the whole community that generate energy even in people who are lazy. And here at Gethsemani we are at the same time Cistercians and Americans. It is in some

---

3. Garden City, NY: Image Books, 1964, p. 9.

respects a dangerous combination. Our energy runs away with us. We go to work like a college football team taking the field. . . . If we want something, we easily persuade ourselves that what we want is God's will just as long as it turns out to be difficult to obtain. What is easy is my own will: what is hard is God's will. And because we make fetishes out of difficulties we sometimes work ourselves into the most fantastically stupid situations, and use ourselves up not for God but for ourselves. We think we have done great things because we are worn out. If we have rushed into the fields or into the woods and done a great deal of damage, we are satisfied.[4]

My wife, Linda, and I have participated in a number of small groups that used the results of standard psychological tests to stimulate spiritual and emotional growth.[5] One of the things these tests revealed about me was a narcissistic streak in my personality. At one time, narcissism was understood as excessive self-love and preoccupation with self. However, recent advances in the psychological understanding of narcissism have shown the problem to be a *lack* of healthy self-love, which, in extreme cases, approaches self-hate.

This has shown up dramatically in my work life. I have talents and aptitudes for solving difficult, complex problems. But I always felt compelled to seek out the most difficult challenges and tackle them in the most difficult way possible. In other words, I have been attracted to self-destructive achievement goals instead of choices based on enlightened self-interest.

As I have become aware of Christ's call to me in the workplace, however, I have realized that this means he calls me to emotional maturity in the work arena. God does give divine order to my life as I learn to accept the work God calls me to (even if it is easy) and go about it in a way that is pleasing to God.

The arena of daily work will continue to test my HEART

---

4. Thomas Merton, *The Signs of Jonas* (New York: Harcourt Brace, 1948).
5. Spiritual growth materials were obtained from Yokefellows, Inc., Burlingame, California, and Glen Reddell, Spiritual Growth Foundation, Lubbock, Texas.

because I (like most other people) am an immature, sinful person working in a world that is basically under the domain of the evil one. But as Christ's person in the world, I am called to responsible obedience to Christ. This means I must continually work at allowing him to reorder the location, the style, and even the motivation for my daily work.

A QUESTION OF MOTIVATION

The second guideline for the arena of work comes from the question: What impact does a developing HEART have on my motivation for work?

For much of my life my motivation was the "American dream," which, as I defined it, was the dream of accumulating enough wealth so that I wouldn't have to work any more! Of course, this would also mean the "good life"—especially material possessions. But this so-called "American dream" is certainly not solely an American phenomenon. The motivation of materialism is an affliction of all cultures, as Michael Maccoby discovered when he examined Swedish society:

> What do the Swedes believe in? Not in organized religion. Some managers and engineers believe in the organization and technology. But most Swedes value the good life as defined by the accumulation of objects, including a car and a summer house. A career is secondary and for many, it is only a necessary nuisance. A combination of high wages for workers, high taxes for managers, and generous social benefits for everyone minimizes career incentives. "We are owned by our possessions," a Swede told me. "The price of labor is so high that you must do everything for yourself, the plumbing, carpentry, and gardening. You spend your time getting things and taking care of them."[6]

If I believe that my daily work is used by God to give divine order to my life, however, my motivation changes. Material things can become instruments in God's hands to

---

6. *The Leader* (New York: Simon & Schuster, 1981), p. 149.

reveal to me my own self-centeredness and self-seeking and the dangers of a life motivated by unrestrained materialism.

In his lectures on Genesis in 1938, Dietrich Bonhoeffer predicted the effects of selfish and materialistic exploitation of the earth and technology on all people:

> We do not rule, we are ruled. The thing, the world, rules man. Man is a prisoner, a slave of the world, and his rule is illusion. Technology is the power with which the earth grips man and subdues him. And because we rule no more, we lose the ground, and then the earth is no longer our earth, and then we become strangers on earth. We do not rule because we do not know the world as God's creation, and because we do not receive our dominion as God-given, but grasp it for ourselves. There is no dominion without serving God.[7]

Bonhoeffer does not condemn technology, but rather a selfish use of technology—one that ignores responsible obedience to God. He is talking about motivation. And the issues have not really changed since Bonhoeffer's time. We have had decades of "hot" and "cold" war, an ever-present nuclear threat, unbelievably high automobile-fatality statistics, industrial disasters, energy crises, and the list goes on. As people use technology to amplify their own sins to enormous proportions, the earth uses technology to hold us captive. For example, the moral and ethical shape of an entire culture can now be shaped by anyone who controls communications.

The struggle of the ordinary Christian in today's high-tech workplace is to be free of being possessed by our possessions and held captive and subdued by technology. But how do we do this? One option is the ancient monastic choice to withdraw from the world. But for us laypeople who are called to follow Christ into the high-tech world, the only other alternative is a change of motivation. *My motivation for daily work must be a desire to serve God as a steward of the earth and a steward of my own talents and aptitudes.* This is the second guideline for daily work.

---

7. *Creation and Fall* (New York: Macmillan, 1959), p. 40.

Such an attitude creates a jolting cultural shock in my personal work arena, where most entrepreneurs and venture capitalists seem to be motivated by a desire for the "big score"—one spectacularly successful business deal that leaves them set for life.

I am fortunate, therefore, to have had as a friend a corporate executive who modeled service and stewardship as a primary motivation for his daily work. John E. Mitchell, Jr., was chairman of the board of a Dallas manufacturing company when I first met him in a Sunday school class he taught. I was fresh out of college, but John treated me like a friend and allowed me to observe how he ran his life and his company. His life showed the marks of a developed HEART as he served his company, the city of Dallas, and his Lord.

Mr. Mitchell had elected to build his company on a principle found in Paul's letter to the Colossian church: "Whatever your task, work heartily, as serving the Lord and not men" (Col. 3:23). I have slowly come to understand the wisdom of living by that verse. For years, I had misread the verse as "whatever your *job*, work heartily." To me, "job" meant all my career aspirations and occupational hopes rolled into one package that extended far into the future. But John Mitchell taught me that a task was something different, just a single stepping stone on the way to my goal. When I learned to focus on the task at hand, my world of daily work took on a new meaning. The task could be high or low, significant or trivial, but God was personally involved. My motivation became the challenge to take each task seriously and attack it with hearty and prayerful enthusiasm, whether or not it contributed to my emotionally charged goals of recognition and achievement. God's therapy and discipline for me is a call to excellence in the ordinary tasks of each day.

John E. Mitchell, Jr., eventually documented his approach to daily work in his book, *The Christian in Business* (the book I mentioned at the beginning of this chapter):

All right-thinking businessmen realize that anyone connected with management of a business is just a servant anyway.

He is a servant of the owner of the business, a servant of the customers, a servant of the employees, a servant of the community, a servant of local governments, a servant of Uncle Sam, a servant of many other people—and if he has the vision to see it and the courage to act upon it, a servant of God.[8]

THE FUTURE IS IN GOD'S HANDS

As I allow God to reshape my motivation with the task at hand, it's almost impossible to resist a glance into the future. Even if I discipline myself to serve God in the tasks that come my way, I still find myself asking where all of this is leading. Am I getting ahead or not? Jobs break down into a sequence of tasks, and careers break down into a sequence of jobs that begin in the past and lead off into the future. So another variation on the original question of the HEART in the workplace is: What impact does a developed HEART have on my future and my career goals?

The answer must lie in the ability of a growing HEART to shape and form career goals. Michael Maccoby describes in *The Gamesman* four main work character types. (I can actually recognize the types when I remember those I left behind at a large multinational electronics company four years ago!) The "craftsman" is motivated by a desire "to do his own thing" and get recognition. I seldom see a "craftsman" change jobs for money, but their simple-yet-comfortable lifestyle is something of a paradox. They may strain to push an old car to two-hundred-thousand miles while "squirreling away" thousands of dollars in the stock market, a farm, or a log home on some distant mountain.

The "company man" is motivated by a need for "corporate" security and a place on the team. Some are content as well-adjusted members of various computer and aerospace projects—the disciplined, loyal, responsible organizational men who hold things together. When chased by a persisting fear of falling behind in the corporate parade,

---

8. *The Christian in Business*, p. 23.

they can sell anything—including themselves—to get to the head of the parade. If this attempt to achieve a career goal fails, they can at times revert to playing out the role of a lonely, submissive bureaucrat.

The "jungle fighter," an increasingly rare bird in corporate life, is often ruthless and driven by a need for power over people. Career goals are simply those "chess moves" within the corporate matrix that preserve or enhance his position of power. I can vividly recall the sickening scene of a desperate "jungle fighter" turning against long-time friends and loyal employees in order to keep from being terminated for managerial incompetence.

The "gamesmen" are those annointed to ascend the steps to corporate leadership in the high-tech age. At their best, they are the innovative, flexible, hardworking winners—and most admired and most successful. This is the man in charge! But as I recall the "gamesmen" I have known, my admiration is often mixed with fear—they cannot be trusted. Their career goals are centered on being winners, not gifted leaders. When their winning goals are not met, I have seen them retreat inside an emotional shell where their lives begin to crumble.

In addition to these four character types described by Maccoby, I have met yet another type in my present work arena of high-tech startup—the entrepreneurs, who are propelled by a compelling need to achieve. Their allies—and often, at the same time, their enemies—are the venture capitalists who control the money and have an enormous need for power. (In an entrepreneurial city like Dallas, people often say that money is not the goal; it is just a way of keeping score.)

A developing HEART can reorder any of these diverse career goals, however, when I am willing to set aside corporate or personal goals to understand God's goals for me in a particular situation. This is risky business because God may give me a place where I can best serve rather than most successfully assert myself. But the third biblical guideline for work is that *I must accept the fact that my unfolding future in my daily work is in God's hands.*

This definitely does not come naturally for me. As I have gone about my training and career, I have often felt that my future was is in a corporation's hands or a university's hands or my customers' hands or even my own hands. But as my HEART has developed over the years, I have gradually been able to turn more and more of my career concerns over to God.

RESPONSIBLE FOR DEVELOPING WHAT GOD GAVE

Even if the future is in God's hands, *I have in my own hands the stewardship responsibility for developing my own talents, aptitudes, and abilities.* This fourth guideline means that God can guide and direct my work life as I work at being a good steward of my personal resources.

Several years ago, at my wife's insistence, I read John Bolles' book, *What Color Is Your Parachute?,*[9] which is now considered a classic in the field of career planning. Linda claimed that I had the problem that afflicts large numbers of people in the work arena—I was underemployed. At the time, I was a new-product development manager at Texas Instruments. They liked me, and I liked them. How could I be underemployed in a major high-technology company?

I found the answer at the AIMS Testing Laboratory, an industrial psychology research institute in Dallas which specializes in aptitude testing. AIMS career guidance is based on an individual's natural aptitudes and God-given abilities (two dozen in all) rather than acquired skills or personal preferences.

There are no good scores or bad scores for the tests given at the AIMS institute. Each pattern of high and low aptitudes points to occupations where people with similar patterns have found satisfaction in their work.

As AIMS researcher Irvin Shambaugh spread the test data before me, he solved a career satisfaction problem that had puzzled me for five years. According to the tests, I was doing the right thing in the wrong place! I had the test pattern

---

9. Berkeley: Ten Speed Press, 1979.

of someone who needs a rich diet of technical and managerial problems to solve. But the higher I progressed up the management ladder in a large corporation, the more I was watching other people solve problems rather than solving them myself. I needed to be in a smaller company or consulting business so that I could solve a wide variety of problems each day.

As I reviewed my test results, I recalled a question from one of Dr. Lloyd Ogilvie's sermons: "What difference would it make in your life if you could see what God had in mind when he created you?" I realized that, in some ways, the list of twenty-one God-given aptitudes suggested by my test results was part of the picture in God's mind. And the AIMS people also assured me that my strong aptitudes that were not developed and used in my work, or at least in a hobby, would frustrate me until my dying day.

If my work aptitudes represent the way God put me together, the issue of the HEART for the arena of daily work is a stewardship issue. How should I develop and invest my aptitudes and skills as an act of responsible obedience to Jesus Christ? If my future is in God's hands, the shape of that future will take form as God guides me in investing my life in the arena of daily work. My next job or position is just a step that allows God to unfold my future.

I would even go so far as to suggest that Satan's strategy for the work arena of the high-tech age may be to lock the laity into work where they are underemployed or misapplying their God-given gifts and aptitudes. Psychologists have discovered that we tend to develop a self-image as a worker in our first job and to carry it with us—true or untrue—for the rest of our career. But as God's people in the high-tech world, we must learn to look to *Christ*—not to some outdated self-image—to learn who we are in the work arena. Under God's guidance and direction, we can then practice Bolles' *Parachute* philosophy, which says that if we know what we do best, what we want to do most, and where we want to do it, we can find an employer or customer who wants it done.

164

WHAT IS SUCCESS?

The final guideline deals with expectations of success, rewards, and prosperity. As I pointed out to my agnostic friend in graduate school, I believe a Christian in business *should* expect to make a profit. But at the same time, the Bible does single out success in the work arena as a potential danger to the HEART.

Through the prophet Ezekiel, God spoke this word very clearly to his people. Ezekiel targeted first the extremely successful merchants and traders in the coastal city of Tyre: "By your great wisdom in trade you have increased your wealth, and your HEART has become proud in your wealth" (Ezek. 28:5). He also compared Egypt in its great success as a nation with a giant stately cedar of Lebanon: "Therefore thus says the Lord God: Because it towered high and set its top among the clouds, and its HEART was proud of its height, I will give it into the hand of a mighty one of the nations" (Ezek. 31:10, 11). Even Israel was described to Ezekiel as a people who will "hear what you say but they will not do it; for with their lips they show much love, but their HEART is set on their gain" (Ezek. 33:31). The Bible is very clear that no amount of personal or corporate success can do away with the need of a developed HEART.

This issue of success and failure in daily work has been a very personal one to me in the last few years. Three years ago, with my AIMS test results in one hand and Bolles' *Parachute* book in the other, I drew a circle on the calendar to mark the day I planned to leave Texas Instruments. Keith Miller and Tom Fatjo introduced me to a stimulating creative dreaming process in their book, *With No Fear of Failure.* [10] I used all of these resources to develop a roadmap for starting my own business. Then, I took the leap.

Now, as I look back over the last few years and ask, "Have I been successful? Has God blessed me?" I find these are difficult questions to answer.

---

10. Waco, TX: Word Books, 1981.

There have been plenty of setbacks. For example, one of my goals was to begin a business manufacturing a new kind of optical filter for lasers. As I began this project, I saw my optical engineer and chief consultant walk away and throw up their hands. I had to return to the laboratory to develop the product myself and find out if it could be built. My three potential customers, all major U.S. corporations, fell on their own spears and failed to win contracts for products that would have used my filter. Our initial funding was for a three-month effort that took a year to complete. After two years, I discovered that just to stay in business I would have to find new customers and develop a new version of the product at my own expense. (This experience is normal for a start-up company.)

I have worked long and late fighting cash-flow problems, meeting technical challenges, and hunting for new customers. And the whole time I have been painfully aware that 50 percent of the new start-up companies like mine fail in the first two years. Only 10 percent remain after five years. So while I am as sure as I can be that this is what God wanted me to *try,* it is really hard to know whether I have been successful.

When I told my story to my friend, Bruce Larson, he summed it up: "You may be a millionaire or you may be broke and you don't even know." That's about the state of things in my business. I have faced the possibility of soaring success and the possibility that the whole project must be abandoned. In either case, I have been forced to open my work life to Christ in prayer as I face my own HEART and my tasks one day at a time.

Looking back, I can see that I began this venture with high hopes and enthusiasm grounded in what is commonly called the "Puritan work ethic"—the belief that if you are industrious and work very hard, God will bless you materially. I owe a debt to Os Guinness[11] for pointing out that a corollary to this belief was that the poor were God's naughty

---

11. I am grateful to Os Guinness for insights into the Puritan work ethic, which he described in a lecture on the subject of Christian vocation.

children who obviously had not worked hard enough to earn God's blessings, and that certain sins—especially sexual impurity—were particularly dangerous and to be avoided at all costs.

Well, the result of the last few years is that I have worked very hard and also avoided sexual sins. And so far the material blessings have not come to pass. Does this mean I am one of God's naughty children? I don't think so.

Guinness also reports that these "Puritan work ethic" ideas came late in the Puritan movement and were actually a marked departure from the thinking of early Puritans as well as from the Bible.

The "work ethic" of these early Puritans was based on Paul's advice to the Colossian church (John E. Mitchell's guideline): Whatever your task, work heartily as serving the Lord, not men. Once they had done their tasks, they believed it was up to God whether and how they were blessed. These early Puritans were careful to share their excess and care for the poor. And the major sin they felt must be avoided at all cost was covetousness—an inordinate desire for wealth and material possessions, especially those belonging to someone else.

It is this *early* "Puritan work ethic," that is the basis of the fifth guideline for the arena of daily work. Simply stated, *it is up to God whether and how I am blessed.* I must accept this for my own business venture even though I have high hopes for the future.

Have I been blessed so far? God has met my needs and the needs of my family. He has skipped over few of our wants these last few years. I have been blessed with daily work that uses my gifts and aptitudes. God has guided me and used my work to give divine order to my life, especially patient endurance. I have been blessed with a sense of Christ's involvement with the tasks that I must perform each day to serve my clients and customers.

The jury is still out on the long-term business growth and profitability of my company. But my work arena has been a successful outpost for spiritual ministry to and counseling of the people I work for and with. I have seen Christ break

167

into my work arena to touch human life with love, forgiveness, and guidance. My work is successful as long as Christ becomes real each day in the arena of my daily work.

I work for and pray toward business success but, once that I have done all I can, I am learning to relax in the knowledge that blessings in terms of profit and loss are ultimately in God's hands.

When I wake in the early morning hours to plan and worry, this knowledge helps me to go back to sleep. This must be part of what Paul meant when he advised his Galatian friends, "Have no anxiety about anything, but in everything by prayer and supplication with thanksgiving let your requests be made known to God. And the peace of God, which passes all understanding, will keep your HEARTs and your minds in Christ Jesus" (Phil. 4:6–7). Maturity of the HEART must mean that I experience the peace of God in my arena of daily work.

When I open the arena of my daily work to Christ and pay the price of discipline to develop my HEART, an amazing thing occurs. Little by little a sense of adventure returns. As the meaning of my work grows, I know that it is satisfying a need for adventure that God has placed in my HEART.

12. The Arena of Marriage and Family

My personal formula for making business air travel as painless as possible calls for signing up for an aisle seat, praying for an empty center seat, and burying myself in new magazines until the meal comes. But then I have to talk. It is impossible for me to eat a meal on an airline without commenting to someone.

One spring night somewhere over Arkansas, American Airlines served a curious Italian dish, and I compulsively broke the silence with a quiet travel companion in the window seat. He was a research psychologist returning to his Ivy League university from a Texas lecture tour. Over dinner, he described some of his research, which was aimed at unraveling the basic mechanisms of depression.

As we talked, my head swirled with images and experiences—flashbacks from the last few years of my marriage. Linda and I had been very much in love when some mysterious "dark force" had attacked our seemingly healthy and happy relationship. This "dark force" cut right through our common faith in Christ and our commitment to each other and dragged us into a hellish nightmare of personal stress and tension. Although I had never been able positively to identify what was happening, I believed that Linda had spiraled into an uncontrollable depression while I stood by feeling helpless. But a professional counselor had not been able to find any signs of depression.

That night as I visited with my dinner companion about the dynamics of depression, his words kicked up my suspicions and past feelings like puffs of wind swirling dry leaves.

Finally, my curiosity finally won out over my hesitancy to open a still-fresh wound. I very casually said that I suspected that my wife had had a problem with depression. I added that a professional counselor had given her a standard psychological test that was computer-graded seventeen different ways and had found no sign of depression. I told him the name of the test.

He showed no surprise. According to him, that particular test "couldn't catch depression in a basket." He had developed a short test of his own to specifically screen for depression. He seemed to read my mind as he took a copy of the test out of his briefcase and offered it to me. "If you want a quick check on your wife's condition, fill this out the way you think she would have answered at the time you suspected the depression. It would only be a guess, but I could give you some indication."

The test was short—only a few pages. As I went to work, each multiple-choice question carried me back to the very darkest days. Somewhere over Tennessee, I finished my pop quiz, cleaned off the tomato sauce, and handed the sheets to my travel companion. He studied it while I started dessert, and finally spoke with a cautious, grave tone. "If a person turned in a score like this, she would fall in the most severely depressed 5 percent of the population. She would most likely need hospitalization and certainly would need the finest professional help available." As he delivered this stern warning, he scribbled out the name of a professor at the University of Texas at Austin who could help me locate the top professional psychologist in Dallas if the problem came back. He made it clear that a person with these scores could suddenly "crash" emotionally and take years to recover.

Then it hit us both at the same time that this was a practice run. He'd never seen the "patient." He asked cautiously, "How is your wife doing now?" I told him that she was much better, and that we seemed to be out of the woods. With a surge of genuine relief and professional curiosity, he asked what I had done to get through this crisis period in our marriage.

My answer described the greatest testing of the HEART I have yet experienced in a relationship with another human being. From our earlier conversation, I sensed that the psychologist was emerging from a sort of atheistic period in his life, so I felt I must warn him that I had relied strongly on spiritual resources and personal faith to get through it and survive.

I realize now that the route I explored trying to save my marriage led me to see the arena of marriage and the family from a new perspective—as a divine mandate. In my struggle with the unnamed "dark force," I was forced to function out of simple obedience to Jesus Christ with no roadmap or master plan.

I see my experiences as a parable for those of us called to obey Christ in our marriages and families in the high-tech age. All around us in the high-tech world, experiments on male-female relationships and family configurations are in process. Those who would follow Christ in the arena of marriage and the family must develop for themselves clear biblical concepts of marriage and family, because the world around us has lost its collective memory of what we are even talking about.

A TROUBLED TIME

I was forced to go to work on this task of redefining marriage when I first noticed a change in Linda right after our child was born. Paul's long-awaited arrival was the most celebrated event in our seven-year marriage, an unexplained victory in a hard-fought fertility battle. But after the excitement died down, stress and tension began to build. People around us seemed to see our situation through their own rose-colored glasses. When we talked about the choppy waters, they gave the standard replies: "Having a baby really changes your life, doesn't it?" and "If you think it's bad now, just wait until. . . ." But if all of this was a joke that would pass, I wondered, why was our relationship deteriorating?

As more and more of our individual needs went unmet,

we withdrew from each other, and Linda withdrew from the people who couldn't hear us or take our problems seriously. Most of the people she wanted to turn to for help were too far away or too weighted down with personal problems of their own. From Linda's perspective, I couldn't support her emotionally, and her world was falling apart. Her spiritual, emotional, and physical tanks were on empty, yet she miraculously rallied her resources each day to function effectively as a mother.

The stress pulled me down as I watched Linda slide into a kind of hopelessness in which she began to believe that Paul and I would be better off without her. Nothing I tried worked. Talk only led us into late-night arguments over unmet personal needs. Small groups that had been supportive in the past responded with, "Oh! You don't really feel that way!" We were leaders to these people, and I sensed their fear and panic when we shared our own problems. (I wonder if these Christians could not acknowledge and face real trouble in the lives of a couple to whom they had looked for leadership because of a fear that, if it could happen to us, it could happen to them.)

After weeks of study, prayer, and thinking, I reached a conclusion. Linda was sliding into an ever-deepening depression and there was nothing I knew to do about it except to get outside help. But when I tried to calmly confront Linda with this fact, she refused to accept it. I dug in my heels and demanded that we get a professional checkup. For all I knew, I could be causing her problems or blocking her recovery. I just had to know if I was right or wrong and figure out what to do about it.

Linda reluctantly showed up for our first session with the counselor and sat quietly as I explained our problem, saying that we loved each other, but that we needed a marriage tune-up because things just weren't running right. After hours of testing, the counselor and his computer cast their votes. I felt that I must be in the wrong meeting: The test detected no noticeable depression in either of us.

I came back a week later with my personal journal and reviewed in detail my suspicions of depression. The counselor listened and rechecked his computer printouts. His vote was still a definite "no" to depression. With a clean bill of mental health, we were sent home to live happily ever after. But the situation continued to deteriorate, and I knew I had to look for some other kind of help.

My first step was to face the fact that I was helpless in a hopeless situation. Genuine despair is justified when the ship is going down, and my feelings were telling me to abandon ship! I never felt more unloved, rejected, and exhausted as my needs went unmet, and Linda and I rapidly lost our ability to communicate. My reserves of courage and endurance were nearly gone. I backed off for one final desperate attempt to pray and think of some course of action.

A FIRST STEP

Finally, the first step came to me: I must focus on understanding Linda at this place in her life. In order to do this, I would need God's help, and I would have to drop my self-righteous demands and grinding defenses of my rights. One thing I did understand was the hidden guilt and nagging fear of failure that she carried with her from the failure of her first marriage. As she increasingly failed to meet her own high standards as wife, mother, and homemaker, the fear of another failure was eating away at her.

With this in mind, I was able to confront her with the truth. No matter what she felt or feared, I was not leaving. We were partners in this marriage and partners in Christ. I had no idea how to fix things and I didn't know a way out of our problems. We were lost in the woods. But we were lost together. Our best choice was to hang on to each other and pray that God would show us the way out. We couldn't help each other, and so we had to fall back on total grace—unmerited love and affection.

I was really leaning on an intriguing concept of how Christians should live together in a community—a subject that had interested me even before I met Linda. And I had come to believe that the basis for this life together was Jesus Christ. He is not only a mediator between God and human beings, but also a mediator between people. Christ in a marriage relationship makes the marriage more than the social experiences of mating, feeding, and migration. My hope was to make our marriage the smallest unit of Christian community—a community of confessed sinners welded together by God's grace and forgiveness.

Hope for marriage and the family in the high-tech age lies in our ability to grasp the concept that our families are to be dynamic Christian communities. The life-changing power of Jesus Christ must be released to transform these relationships.

I must see my wife and children as Christ sees them: practicing sinners saved by grace, not servants sent to make my life ideal. Christ calls me to serve them as brothers and sisters in a tiny segment of the body of Christ, the church. As Christ becomes real to me in this arena, I am freed to venture beyond the boundaries of traditional romantic love and feelings.

THE COST OF COMMITMENT

I had no idea what the cost would be for my renewed commitment to Linda, but the first step promised to be very expensive; it would cost me my time. As a creative workaholic, I could easily fill up my days with lectures, teaching, conferences, committees, and directorships that all looked like worthwhile projects. But axing away these outside commitments and regulating the amount of time that I would invest in my career was my only way to find more time to be with Linda. My deep-felt professional needs to achieve, to be respected, and to be accepted had to be put on hold, because in order for me to understand and eventually help Linda we had to spend time together. And this was very hard for me.

As un-Christian as it sounds, being helpful and supportive goes against the grain of my personality. At least, Linda and I had learned early in our marriage that we were uniquely mismatched in this area. Psychological testing had shown Linda's "felt need" for personal encouragement and sympathy to be stronger than 98 percent of the general population. At the same time, I had discovered that my "felt need" to reach out and spontaneously *give* encouragement and sympathy put me in the bottom 1 percent. We were so useless to each other according to the tests that all we could do was laugh about the test results.

I knew that what I naturally felt like doing for Linda was not enough. So I began to pray that Christ would free me and give me the strength to reach out in love to Linda at the points where her needs were the greatest, even if it went against my ingrained personality patterns.

Through this dark passage in my marriage, I faced the fact that I tended to use my consuming interests in my work, my church, and the community to avoid responsibilities to my wife and family. I still do, but Christ continually calls me to balance my life in these four areas as an act of obedience to him.

Once I accept the arena of marriage and the family as divinely mandated, I must ask what it means to be Christ's person in this arena. When I approach this area in responsible obedience to Jesus Christ, I am challenged at the level of the HEART. The priorities accepted by the high-tech world around me no longer apply. The reality of a growing, developing HEART must propel me to responsible service to my wife and family that may carry me far beyond the comfort zone of my own personality. I cannot use the high-tech world as a place to hide from my wife and family.

THE CALL TO LEADERSHIP

At the time, what I wanted most was to withdraw into my own isolated world and hope that all my problems would be gone when I emerged. I had followed this passive pattern of reacting instead of responding in love all of my life. But I knew that my family needed leadership, not someone sitting quietly waiting for the problems to go away.

As I continued to pray for guidance, I began to see my family as a tiny Christian community, almost like the monastic communities I had read about in the writings of

Bonhoeffer and St. Benedict. We were stuck with each other—Linda and Paul were the "monks," and I was the "abbot." So I worked out a plan to get us organized on that pattern. First, I called everyone together at the breakfast table each morning for a reading of one chapter of the Old Testament and one-half chapter of the New Testament. And I began the ancient practice of prayer by the abbot each morning for the specific needs of each monk. The abbot must pray without asking the monk for a need list, which means the abbot must keep in touch with the lives of his monks on a daily basis.

Because Linda and I were stumped on both the problem and its solution, at first our prayer was simply, "Lord, deliver us from things seen and unseen and show us what you would have us do." We didn't really expect an instantaneous, miraculous fix, and none came. But as the days passed, we gradually began to sense God's presence. So far, we had no answers, but we knew Christ was in our painful situation with us. We knew we weren't alone!

The message for the high-tech age from this "meeting of the monks" is that the family needs leadership and discipline as a Christian community. It is totally counter to my personality to want to make time and put out the effort to provide that leadership. But I reached the point that I either had to lead or risk losing my wife. The options for the high-tech age are exactly the same—lead or risk losing your wife and family. I reluctantly accepted the fact that Christ calls for responsible obedience within marriage and the family just as he does in the other three arenas of the external strategy.

LEARNING TO MEET NEEDS

In the meantime, I was grinding through books such as Cecil G. Osborne's *The Art of Understanding Your Mate*[1] and Paul Tournier's *To Understand Each Other*,[2] searching

---

1. Grand Rapids: Zondervan, 1970.
2. Richmond, VA: John Knox, 1968.

for some clue to Linda's real needs and ways to respond in love. Then, on my birthday, Linda presented me with one more book in this series called *What Wives Wish Their Husbands Knew About Women.*[3] Her inscription meant more than the gift: "Bob—Some birthday gift, huh? But I really do love you!"

When I noticed from the forward that the book was written by Dr. James Dobson for wives, not husbands, I put it aside for months. When I finally picked it up, I discovered that Dobson's subject was the ten major sources of depression in American women. I flew through the book and realized that Linda was losing the battle against eight of the ten depression-producing problems Dobson had identified over his years of counseling.

When I finished the book, my first impulse was to slam it into Linda's hands and tell her to go fix her life, then come get me when she was well. But the solutions Dobson suggested for the problem of depression contained one more test of the HEART for *me:* Not a single solution was workable by the wife alone. Each trail out of the woods required the husband and wife to walk it together. The cost of helping Linda get better had grown until the task now demanded the most expensive thing I had—the gift of myself.

Dobson's study identified the loss of self-worth as the number-one source of depression in women. I had to learn how to give Linda affirmation and recognition, something that is very difficult for me. Day after day, I saw her crushed by fatigue and time pressure just from the daily grind. Sometimes I could start working to help her. Other times, I had to work out a special strategy, such as arranging to get her away from Paul at least one day a week for rest and relaxation. I began to understand Linda's need to make a place for herself in the world of adults beyond the stressful demands of a preschooler. Linda and I had to build our life together in the world of real people.

Nothing on Linda's list of needs was more difficult for me to face than her need for more romantic love in the

---

3. Wheaton: Tyndale, 1975.

marriage. I was slow accepting this need and the fact that my not meeting the need could be having a depressing effect on her. To accept her feelings as normal, I had to crawl over my own feelings of being judged and rejected, and I had to admit I was guilty of not expressing my love for Linda in ways that she needed to receive it. But I determined to work on this problem. And slowly we set out again to claim and develop the intimacy in our marriage as a gift from God.

A MIRACLE OF THE HEART

I finished this story as the plane prepared to land. I said to the psychologist in the window seat, "That's about all the story. Linda and I both are doing a lot better, even though we still have a long way to go."

He sat quietly for a moment as I waited for his professional opinion. Finally, he said, "That's a miracle."

I had expected a technical, not a theological, opinion. "What's a miracle?" I asked. He went on to explain that, without any professional help, I had done exactly what he or the most competent psychologist would have told me to do. He explained, "It's a miracle you got through it without any professional help." (However, he also gave me a lecture on the seriousness of the problem and the need for top professional help if it recurred.)

I couldn't argue with his diagnosis. Part of the miracle was the growth of my HEART. Part of the miracle was that Christ had met Linda and me in this darkness and had given us the gift of each other and himself for healing.

My dinner partner in the window seat had put his finger on the key to success in the arena of marriage and family for the high-tech age. It takes a miracle. It takes the miracle of Jesus Christ as a mediator between two marriage partners. It takes the miracle of HEARTs growing toward maturity. It takes the miracle of Christ's presence in this tiny family outpost of the body of Christ bringing love, encouragement, and forgiveness.

178

A CALL TO VIGILANCE

It also takes eternal vigilance against threats to the marriage and the family from the world that has lost its collective memory of Christian marriage and the home. The high-tech world has demonstrated the awesome power to use its electronic media to erase from the mind Christ's call to the arena of marriage and the family. Eternal vigilance means learning to identify and defend against the natural enemies of marriage and the family, which are actually enemies of the HEART. Christian families are not granted diplomatic immunity against these enemies. Alcohol abuse, drug abuse, sexual and physical abuse, and a whole array of serious mental-health problems are not respecters of persons who have committed their lives to Jesus Christ. Obedience to Christ demands that I be open to the idea that it *can* happen to me.

As ordinary Christians in the high-tech age, we are confronted with the three very human experiences of divorce, adultery, and fornication. The unusual aspect of this confrontation is that the high-tech world is no longer opposed to these three destructive human activities or even neutral toward them. Recreational sex and divorce have become a national industry, both as a media event and as spectator and participator sports. The power of TV, movies, music, and peer pressure to promote these activities is awesome. The Christian community has been blown apart without even knowing what has hit it as marriages crumble and recreational sex outside marriage among teens and preteens, as well as adults, reaches epidemic levels.

The mention of any of the three topics today sets off heated debates among secular sociologists and Christians with varied viewpoints. But it can be with little debate that divorce, fornication, and adultery are natural enemies of marriage and the family. And I have never met anyone who claimed that he destroyed a marriage, engaged in an affair, or pushed his children into recreational sex outside of marriage intentionally because of responsible obedience to Jesus Christ. But in the high-tech age, when things happen,

179

there is a tendency to blame "the world" and assume no responsibility for letting it happen.

Now, I have not singled out divorce, adultery, and fornication because I think they are the "worst" sins or unforgivable ones. On the contrary, I believe that Christ can call people to himself as never before through these broken relationships, and that he offers new starts to anyone who will accept his forgiveness. Rather, I have focused on these three because they are so destructive to relationships in a marriage and family. Whereas individual, personal sins tend to resemble Murphy's Law, which says, "Anything that can go wrong, will," the relational sins that threaten marriage and the family more resemble Zilche's Principle, a generalization of Murphy's Law, which says, "Anything that can go wrong will go wrong in such a way as to inconvenience the largest number of people."

The difference, of course, is that the damage done by these sins goes far deeper than "inconvenience." It is critical, therefore, that the church in the high-tech age be able to make a positive statement about this threat and to practice preventive medicine.

QUESTIONS OF THE HEART

Christ's teachings on these three subjects are basically the same: He was against all three, and he taught that all three are issues of the HEART. When the Pharisees questioned Christ about divorce, they asked about law—questioning whether divorce was legal based on the commandments of Moses. But Jesus held to his point that divorce was not a legal issue but a matter of the HEART:

> But Jesus said to them, "For your hardness of HEART he wrote you this commandment. But from the beginning of creation, God made them male and female. For this reason a man shall leave his father and mother and be joined to his wife, and the two shall become one. So they are no longer two but one. What therefore God has joined together, let not man put asunder" (Mark 10:5–9).

In this passage, Christ was pointing to marriage as a creative work of God. For Christians, two lives with HEARTs indwelt by Jesus Christ are joined together in a bond that is to be the most stable and permanent element of Christian community. Hardness of HEART is an exercise of the will to override God's will for two people in the body of Christ and destroy God's creative work. (Looking at divorce this way, as a matter of the HEART and an issue in the body of Christ makes no sense at all to the high-tech world.)

Adultery was presented to Christ as a physical issue. But again he held that it is an issue of the HEART:

> You have heard that it was said, "You shall not commit adultery." But I say to you that every one who looks at a woman lustfully has already committed adultery with her in his HEART. If your right eye causes you to sin, pluck it out and throw it away; it is better that you lose one of your members than that your whole body be thrown into hell. And if your right hand causes you to sin, cut it off and throw it away; it is better that you lose one of your members than that your whole body go into hell (Matt. 5:27–30).

I am not aware of any Christian group today that practices amputation as a rite to promote sinless living—sexual or otherwise. And I don't think that is what Jesus was advocating. His point was that adultery comes from the HEART and grows out of the intellect, will, and emotions—blanking out spiritual and ethical values.

Jesus puts the role of the HEART in perspective by comparing an expanded list of problems of the HEART with Jewish rituals and ordinances:

> "Do you not see that whatever goes into a man from outside cannot defile him, since it enters, not his HEART but his stomach, and so passes on?" [Thus he declared all foods clean.] And he said, "What comes out of a man is what defiles a man. For from within, out of the HEART of man, come evil thoughts, fornication, theft, murder, adultery, coveting, wickedness, deceit, licentiousness, envy, slander, pride, foolishness. All these evil things come from within, and they defile a man" (Mark 7:18–23).

181

The sexual sins of fornication and adultery fall in Jesus' list on either side of theft and murder. The issue is not the degree of seriousness, but the fact that all items on the list are matters of the HEART and are prevented by developing the HEART to the required level of maturity for faithful obedience to Jesus Christ. The greatest friend of marriage and the family is a developed HEART. Unfortunately, the church cannot offer much hope to the high-tech world in the arena of marriage and family until it gets its own act together. People continue to do what you do, not what you say.

A TESTING OF THE HEART

Perhaps, the problem that I faced in my own marriage would have been easier to accept and understand if I had known that God uses the arena of marriage for testing the HEART. Linda and I both shared a common faith in Jesus Christ, and our wedding was a joyous commitment of our lives to one another in Christ. Before meeting Linda, I had always had a mental image of my eventual marriage partner as a freshly scrubbed sorority coed straight off a college campus. Instead, Linda came to me straight out of a standard American tragedy—a divorce from a young dentist who walked out the front door when he finished dental school. I had my doubts about marrying someone who had been married before, but I tried to be honest with God in seeking his guidance. And the response I sensed God giving me was the terse, direct reply given to the balky Peter, a pious Jew, who was asked by God in a dream to eat food forbidden under Jewish law: "Don't call unclean that which God calls clean." From then on, I knew that, though she was divorced, what mattered was that Linda had found the Christ who loved and cared more for her than I ever would or could.

As I look back at our encounter with the dark force of depression, I wonder if I needed healing more than Linda. Dr. Paul Tournier explains what I now believe happened to me:

> As long as a man is preoccupied primarily with being understood by his wife, he is miserable, overcome with self-pity,

182

the spirit of demanding and bitter withdrawal. As soon as he becomes preoccupied with understanding her, and with his own wrongdoing in not having understood her, the direction taken by events begins to change. . . . To find the key to understanding, the secret of living—This is an inner experience, a discovery, a conversion and not simply acquisition of new knowledge . . . it is a rather insignificant happening which strikes him, a word, an encounter, a death, a recovery, a look, or a natural event. God uses such to reach a man.[4]

This experience *is* a miracle that somehow let me see our marriage through the filter of my HEART.

---

4. *To Understand Each Other,* p. 59.

13. The Arena of Government

A few months ago, I represented the high-tech community on a panel which met for a two-day round-table discussion of present and future issues facing the church. One session focused on the topic of government and the church, and began a vigorous discussion of politics. And I began to wish I was somewhere else.

I have a thorough dislike for politics, which may come from growing up in Oklahoma. The major political issues that I remember from my childhood and adolescence are the votes to legalize alcoholic beverages, the speculation on the length of time before more state Supreme Court justices were impeached, the news about the next bootlegger to get a jail term and the latest "pork barrel" trophy to be dragged home from Washington to build a new lake or dig a river. I mentally withdrew from the panel discussion to wait impatiently for a "juicy" high-tech topic.

Finally, after nearly half an hour, the present-and-future-issues group gradually shifted from *politics* to *government.* And a light bulb went on for me. A side effect of my distaste for politics has been an attitude that said to leave the politics to someone else. But I now realized that I often confuse politics and government, and that I might have been guilty over the years of leaving the *government* to someone else.

I'm still not crazy about politics. My knowledge and experience in this arena would make up a short chapter. But the issue I want to address here is not politics, but the arena of government and the impact of a developing HEART on responsible obedience to Christ in this arena.

CALLED TO THE ARENA OF GOVERNMENT

As I began to research this subject, I realized that I had been involved professionally in both politics and government for quite a while. For nearly twenty years, I have been involved in defense contracting and federally sponsored research and development. I have been involved in the government of the Presbyterian church as an elder. Last, but not least, I am a citizen of a country with a government by the people.

I was embarrassed to realize that I do not always readily associate my personal faith in Christ with my responsibilities in government. But my HEART convinced me that, if the arena of government is a divine mandate, I am called to sharpen my understanding, skills, and participation in this arena out of obedience to Christ.

Part of my rationalization for neglecting the arena of government over the years has come from my knowledge that, *in the end,* the things of this world do not matter for those who know Jesus Christ. But increasingly my journey of the HEART has forced me to take a fresh look at the biblical record. And I have come to realize that, *until the end,* the things of this world matter a great deal. The Bible makes it clear that God is genuinely concerned about how we live together in communities, nations, and as a global community—as evidenced by the divine mandate for government.[1]

But what is the exact nature of God's concern? The answer must be revealed in the biblical description of government and God's expectations for government. Since I do not pretend to be a political scientist, it is fortunate that the biblical concepts of government are simple enough that I can understand them and gain insight into what it means to follow Christ in the arena of government.

In the biblical framework, government represents a concept of power—the human power to bring order out of chaos and maintain that order. A simple example of this process

---

1. Many of the fundamental ideas on government in this chapter were derived from Dietrich Bonhoeffer's uncompleted manuscript published under the title, *Ethics* (New York: Macmillan, 1965).

at work is the classic Western movie. Westerns are at their best when they dramatize the transition of a local government from chaos to order—just in the nick of time. The small frontier town is overrun with nasty outlaws. While the terrified townsfolk are held captive, a mysterious gunfighter (Gary Cooper or Clint Eastwood—your choice) appears out of the dust and pins the SHERIFF badge to his vest. Three hangings and a big "showdown" gunfight later, law and order is restored.

In the biblical view of this drama, there are only two main types of players: the ruling authorities and those under the authorities (both citizens and noncitizens). We must ask what God expected from the ruling authorities and what he expected from citizens and noncitizens. I believe it is helpful to concentrate on these individual roles before looking at the more complex situation of democratic, self-governing nations, wherein the roles of citizen and ruling authority are combined.

THE RESPONSIBILITIES OF THE GOVERNED

Paul, who lived at a time when neither the Jewish nation nor the Roman Empire were Christian or democratic, wrote to the church at Rome:

> Let every person be subject to the governing authorities. For there is no authority except from God, and those that exist have been instituted by God. Therefore he who resists the authorities resists what God has appointed . . . (Rom. 13:1–2).

It is important to remember that Paul was writing at a time when citizens (not to mention noncitizens) had no responsibility for governing; that responsibility fell entirely on the rulers. Therefore, according to Paul, the primary responsibility of the governed—both citizens and noncitizens—was to obey the ruling authorities as they maintained order. Here Paul was echoing guidelines that Jesus (a noncitizen in the Roman Empire) had given when he told his followers to "render unto Caesar the things that are Caesar's and to God the things that are God's."

But there are other issues involved here. In addition to urging Christians to submit to the authority of government, Paul (like Jesus) was emphasizing the idea that government and church have different functions and must be separate. The different functions of the church and government and the responsibilities of the governed can be clearly established. Paul was saying that all governments draw their power to rule from God and are under the dominion of Jesus Christ (whether they know it or not). Although church and government are separate from each other, both are accountable to God.

Incidentally, although he urged obedience to the government, Paul was never shy about exercising his *rights* as a citizen of the Roman Empire. A citizen—unlike a noncitizen—has rights and duties appointed by the government and is expected to exercise the rights as well as carry out the duties. The value of Paul's citizenship was apparent after he spent a night in a Philippi jail cell and complained heatedly of the unfair treatment he had received:

> "They have beaten us publicly, uncondemned, men who are Roman citizens, and have thrown us into prison; and do they now cast us out secretly? No! Let them come themselves and take us out." The police reported these words to the magistrates, and they were afraid when they heard that they were Roman citizens; so they came and apologized to them (Acts 16:37–39).

WHAT GOD EXPECTS OF GOVERNMENTS

For Paul and Jesus, whose governments gave no ruling responsibilities to citizens and noncitizens, the issue of following Christ in the arena of government was relatively simple—a matter of recognizing and obeying those God has put in authority.

But for those of us who live in a self-governing democracy, the situation becomes far more complicated. We are not only the *governed* but the *government*—the ruling authority. So we must not only ask what is expected of us as citizens under the power of a ruling authority. We must plunge ahead and ask what God expects of those who hold governing power.

In order to understand the divine charter for government, it must be seen as set apart from the other three divinely mandated arenas. A government may regulate work, but it doesn't *do* work. A government may witness and record marriages, but it doesn't perform in a marriage. The church, not the government, is commanded to witness to Jesus Christ as Lord and Savior of his people and call the entire world to fellowship with Christ.

The charter for government is *to establish and maintain order.* It does not create anything and cannot produce life and values. By contrast, the creative power of God is at work in the arenas of work, marriage, and the church. Government is assigned the task of preserving and maintaining that which God has created. The government must recognize the other three arenas and make laws to preserve God's creative work in each arena. And it must secure respect for these laws by enforcement—even by physical force, if necessary.

Built into the biblical charter for government is the assumption that the gospel of Jesus Christ is given free passage within the government's realm. The biblical concern is not to make the government religious or a servant of the church, but rather to see to it that this charter is carried out. Bonhoeffer describes the situation this way:

> Government is instituted for the sake of Christ, it serves Christ and consequently it serves the Church. Yet the dominion of Christ over all government does not imply the dominion of the Church over the government.[2]

The Bible shows no bias toward any particular form of government. The biblical concern is with *what* is to be done, not with *how* it is organized and structured politically. As

---

2. Bonhoeffer, *Ethics,* pp. 346–347.

a citizen of the United States, my pride in our form of government lies in the ability of this system to fulfill the biblical mandate for government. It seems that the ultimate task of those (we) who govern is to see to it that the government is true to the tasks spelled out in the biblical charter and to acknowledge that the power to govern comes from God.

A CASE STUDY IN GOVERNING

As ordinary citizens in a self-governing democracy, we need a practical approach to participation in the divinely mandated arena of government. So I want now to turn to a case study that covers some of the best and some of the worst aspects of the use of governing power.

I would like to examine the life of a certain high-level government executive who rose to top leadership positions and achieved worldwide recognition as a servant leader. He was characterized by a developed HEART and blended organizational know-how with a mastery of technology. As his spiritual development progressed, he spoke openly of his faith in God and publicly acknowledged that he turned to God in prayer to face the great challenges and crises before him. During his rise to national prominence, he made significant contributions in government, defense contracting, agriculture, military leadership, construction, and literature.

As stories go, this man's personal life made a Texas-sized story of soaring success, personal tragedy, and political maneuvering. His early life reads like the script from a nighttime soap opera: A youngest son who took over his dying father's empire after bloody battles with his father's enemies and his older brothers. A dramatic sense of destiny surfaced when he believed that he was picked by his father and chosen by God to complete the one great project his father dreamed of but was never able to start. In fact, he did complete the project with a team of a hundred thousand people and at the cost of an estimated ten billion dollars. This great success ushered in a golden age that allowed him to grow in personal power for forty years.

The subject of this case study is Solomon, king of Israel,

who took the throne at the death of his father, David. Solomon emerges out of the Old Testament record a thousand years before Christ as a leader and manager of a complex, technology-based national economy with an intricate overlay of financial, political, and human problems. At age twenty, this youngest son of Bathsheba successfully fought his brothers for David's throne. The project that David had planned for and that Solomon completed was a home for God, the great temple at Jerusalem. Although he lived three thousand years before the age of high technology, Solomon was forced to manage the industries and technologies of iron, bronze, gold, silver, quarry mining, forestry, gemstones, structural materials, architecture, and military engineering to bring this huge project to fruition.

THE SECRET OF SOLOMON'S SUCCESS

Solomon carved a permanent place for himself in the history of national leadership. His image is that of one who developed the HEART and used his great knowledge and wisdom to work under God for the good of the people he governed. (In fact, Solomon's strong press as a leader often masks the tragic turn made at the end of his career—I will return to this.) I believe that the process at work to shape Solomon's life and perception of the world is the key to effective service in the arena of government today.

When Solomon discovered that he would actually become king, he headed for a retreat in the hills at Gibeon to worship God and get his marching orders straight. In this retreat setting, God put an intriguing management question to Solomon: Do you have everything you need to do your job?

God said, "Ask what I shall give you." The popular tradition is that Solomon asked for wisdom, but the Revised Standard Version translates Solomon's response as, "Give thy servant therefore an understanding mind to govern thy people, that I may discern between good and evil; for who is able to govern this thy great people?" (1 Kings 3:5, 9). Solomon's actual response to God in this vision was *leb shomea,* a Hebrew phrase that literally means "a hearing HEART."

(This is one example where *mind* is used to translate the Hebrew concept of the HEART into English.)

In God's opinion, Solomon came up with the right answer. And God not only answered the prayer of "a mere child, unskilled in leadership" by granting a hearing HEART; he also responded with wealth and honor that lifted Solomon above the international leaders of his world.

Solomon's prayer for a hearing HEART is a model prayer for all who govern or participate in the arena of government. In the increasingly complex government arena of the high-tech age, this prayer is a cry for help in gaining God's insight and finding the courage to act on the knowledge that God gives. Solomon exercised his intellectual and ethical dimensions as he tried to discern and recognize good and evil. And as he prayed for God's guidance, he gave witness as a national leader that he acknowledged the spiritual dimensions of his leadership role.

The prayer of Solomon sets the standard for the laity's participation in the arena of government. The level of involvement and the specific issues will vary, but there is always the need for the HEART to hear God and respond. The call to lay men and women in the high-tech age—whether they are high government officials or citizens casting a single vote—is to enter the arena of government with hearing HEARTs.

A STUDY IN EMERGING LEADERSHIP

A second, less obvious, lesson is also found in the case study of Solomon. Solomon's career is a classic study in emerging leadership. Among the laity today, those who will be tomorrow's leaders may appear today as the most unlikely prospects to respond to Christ's call to solve problems. They come with no apparent resources for the task.

Of the sons of David, Solomon was last in line to be king when he was called. He didn't volunteer, but was picked by a sponsor. The great vision that he made a reality belonged to someone else; the great temple had been David's idea.

All of Solomon's resources also came from someone else. David had kicked in his life's savings and the nation's wealth. The people came through with the rest of the financing once they caught the vision. Even Solomon's great personal leadership skills and abilities were gifts from God in the form of a hearing HEART. (Although I'm sure I would never have wanted Solomon's job, with that kind of backing, I might at least have considered it!)

All in all, Solomon was an unlikely candidate for the job. But his progression to servant leadership in the arena of government represents a pattern I have seen repeated time after time in the case of ordinary lay men and women who are serious about following Christ wherever he leads. Those who eventually emerge as effective lay leaders are quite often unlikely prospects who receive their call through a "second party"—a sponsor, mentor, or friend.

THE TURNING OF A HEART

The case study of Solomon's career has one final point for all who serve Christ in the arena of government and institutions of the high-tech age. Even those God has called and guided in positions of leadership can turn away from him at any time. Unfortunately, Solomon proved that a hearing HEART does not make a person exempt from this pitfall.

When Israel was well into a golden age under Solomon's leadership, his personal power declined and his national organization weakened. His HEART, which had been his strength, had become his problem:

> And the Lord was angry with Solomon, because his HEART had turned away from the Lord, the God of Israel, who had appeared to him twice, and had commanded him concerning this thing, that he should not go after other gods; but he did not keep what the Lord commanded. Therefore the Lord said to Solomon, "Since this has been your mind and you have not kept my covenant and my statutes which I have commanded you, I will surely tear the kingdom from you and will give it to your servant" (1 Kings 11:9–11).

Solomon made the transition from a *hearing* HEART to a *turned* HEART. Country music songwriter Tom T. Hall quite unintentionally caricatures Solomon's decline in his ballad, "Faster Horses." In it, a young philosopher begs and badgers an old, weather-beaten, bowlegged cowboy into telling him the true meaning of life, and the old cowboy sums it up in one line: "It's faster horses, younger women, older whiskey, and more money."[3]

It looks suspiciously like Tom T.'s cowboy was the adviser to Solomon's court. Solomon developed an extravagant lifestyle centered around accumulating horses, new wives, and personal wealth, while Israel's national religion drifted toward an insipid idolatry that involved vigorous religious activity but left God out.

Solomon not only turned away from God and toward Egyptian horses, foreign women, and acquisition of personal wealth (all of which are specifically forbidden under Jewish law for the king of Israel); in the end, Solomon so overtaxed the people to support these pursuits that rebellion destroyed the nation. Solomon's failure as a governing authority finally came because he failed to maintain economic order.

CHALLENGE OF A HEARING HEART

The Bible clearly sets forth the responsibilities of both the ruling authorities and those who come under that authority—two roles which must now merge for those of us in a high-tech democracy. In addition, the specific example of Solomon provides insight into the *hearing* HEART as a key resource for effective governing in all ages. Solomon provides a vivid example, as well, of a governmental disaster brought on by a *turned* HEART—a HEART turned off to God's guidance and counsel. This brings us to the question of what God requires of us in the arena of government.

As I look around me, I see a terrifying array of governmental problems facing the United States at this moment—crises

---

3. Tom T. Hall, "Faster Horses (The Cowboy and the Poet)," Hallnote Music (BMI), © 1976 Phonogram, Inc.

in Central America, fierce competition in the international marketplace, threats of nuclear wars, crime, conflict over abortion, fear of an AIDS epidemic, threat of federal budget disaster—the list goes on and on. High-technology problems and solutions are woven throughout the government fabric. I cannot pretend to offer solutions to these mind-boggling problems. But I believe their solutions must be doggedly pursued by ordinary Christians with hearing HEARTs in response to Christ's call.

But what form will Christ's call take beyond the call to be obedient participants in the governments over us? I believe that one type of call has to do with urging the government to recognize that its authority to govern comes from God. A second type of call comes where the government has failed to establish and maintain order. And a third type of call comes when the government fails to recognize and preserve God's creative handiwork in the arenas of work, family, or the church.

CALLED TO WITNESS TO CHRIST'S DOMINION

The call to witness to the dominion of Jesus Christ over all government immediately raises the flag on the issue of separation of church and state. At the present time in the United States, a number of Christian special-interest groups are taking a variety of approaches to influence laws and public policy. In many cases, no consensus exists between segments of the Christian community on either the goals or the methods. Individuals may become aligned with these special groups because of a charismatic leader, a doctrinal statement, or a particular issue. In such a complex situation, how can I call the government to acknowledge that it is under the dominion of Jesus Christ and still preserve the separation of church and state that is a foundational concept of the Constitution?

If our call is not to make the government "Christian" in a political sense or dominate the government with the church, what is it? I believe our task is to urge the whole world—government included—to submit to the dominion of Jesus Christ. There is always the possibility that those in authority will not heed this urging; indeed, many governments throughout history have chosen to ignore it and have persecuted those who proclaimed the lordship of Christ. And we are not called to *force* anyone to acknowledge Christ. But the alternative to proclaiming Christ's dominion in the arena of government is to submit by default to the dark ruler of this world!

Again Paul provides the model for carrying out such a task. On trial before King Agrippa, Paul told the story of his life-changing encounter with Jesus Christ. The Roman ruler Festus then shouted that Paul's learning had turned him mad. But with his freedom on the line, Paul pressed for acceptance of Jesus as the Christ:

> And Agrippa said to Paul, "In a short time you think to make me a Christian!" And Paul said, "Whether short or long, I would to God that not only you but also all who hear me this day might become such as I am—except for these chains" (Acts 26:28–29).

A warning must be issued at this point, however. The call to urge governments to acknowledge the dominion of Christ can only be met with a developed HEART, because the pressures on those who proclaim Christ to those in authority can be tremendous. (Peter's denial of Christ came when pressed during a government investigation.)

CALLED TO STEP IN WHEN GOVERNMENT FAILS

The second call comes when the government fails to establish and maintain order and we are asked to step in. Ordinary people emerge as leaders because their HEARTs are captured by a vision that must be met out of obedience to Christ.

During the 1930s in Denmark, an internationally recognized lawyer passed through a personal crisis and turned the management of his life over to Jesus Christ. Real spiritual growth continued for several years as Christ gave a new shape to his personal life. In a conversation with the leader of an international Christian lay movement, Valdemar Hvidt asked this spiritual guide what came next. He was answered with a question: "What is the greatest need or problem you are aware of?"

Hvidt cited the problem of unemployment in Denmark because the country was in the grip of the Great Depression. The leader then suggested that Hvidt go try to solve that problem. Considering the disastrous condition of the Danish economy, it was a bizarre suggestion to give to one man.

But Hvidt contacted a few associates, and they began to meet and pray for God's guidance. The government consisted of a bureaucratic mix of socialists and capitalists who were constantly fighting among themselves and had been unable to make a dent in the country's problems. But Hvidt and his team went to work on groups that had never cooperated on anything before. They obtained pledges of cooperation from the prime minister, the Manufacturers Association, the labor unions, and the Chambers of Commerce. After one year, these diverse groups formed the National Organization to Combat Unemployment.

Over the next few years, the employment needs of the country were surveyed and employment plans developed. Farmers listed their needs for improvements, such as irrigation and repairs; unions agreed to work their members at subscale wages; and the government made available low-cost financing. New businesses were started. Bicycle repair centers were set up on the great bicycle parking lots used by nearly every worker who commuted to work, and entrepreneurial repairmen fixed bikes while people were at work.

Great progress was made until the Nazi occupation of Denmark in 1939, when the country fell into a far darker and deeper hole than unemployment. But then Hvidt's team moved on to a new assignment as part of the Christian Resistance Movement against the Nazis. He later served on an international team investigating Nazi war crimes.

I heard Hvidt's amazing story from Howard Blake, founder of the Servant Society, at a recent seminar on the role of the laity in the church. Howard knows Hvidt and was present in Denmark during that time because of his work with the Oxford Group. I verified with Howard that Hvidt had been moved by God to take on a task that had very little probability of success in the world's eyes.

When the government of Denmark was unable to carry out its divine mandate to preserve order in the arena of work and labor, God issued a call to Hvidt, a layman with a growing, hearing HEART. The team and the resources fell into place under God's guidance. As lay men and women develop a strategy for ministry in the high-tech age, they may find, often to their total shock and surprise, that they are emerging government leaders because they were obedient to Christ's call.

THE CALL TO COSTLY OBEDIENCE

The third type of call comes when the government fails to recognize, respect, and protect God's creative work in the arenas of family, work, or church. And this is a call that can have costly consequences for those who dare to obey it.

I visited recently with a mother of grade-school-aged children in public school. She had carefully observed the situation in her children's classrooms and noticed a critical, competitive spirit that was already taking its toll on the children. God placed on her a burden for that class of kids, although she was worried that others would laugh at her concern. With great fear and trembling, she approached several other mothers with the idea of meeting once a week to pray for the children and the class. To her surprise, the mothers accepted her invitation and a prayer group formed that has been a tremendous support as each family has faced problems and crises. Eventually, these mothers used their small group to reach out and witness to other women in the neighborhood.

Public education is the nearest and most visible form of government in most neighborhoods. Christ called the first mother to step out to meet a problem at the risk of personal rejection. And God honored her obedience.

Some calls, however, carry a higher price tag. Many times in this book I have mentioned that I owe a great debt to the German pastor and theologian Dietrich Bonhoeffer for his tremendous insight into the role of Christians in the church and the world. But I also honor him as a man who paid a great personal price for his obedience to God in the arena of government. Bonhoeffer was the son of a prominent Berlin physician whose rise to theological prominence paralleled Hitler's rise to power in Germany. And almost from the beginning, the young pastor and theologian was outspoken in his opposition to the Nazis. In 1933, Bonhoeffer tore into the German public in a radio lecture for longing for a "leader" who was intent on becoming an idol. (He was talking about Hitler.) Bonhoeffer accepted a call to serve German congregations in England rather than have any part of the compromise between the German church and the Nazi government. He visited the United States in 1939, and his friends urged him to stay. But one evening, he listened to a sermon on "Oneness with Christ," and that night, decided to return to Germany, where he worked at tasks for the Resistance and the underground Confessing Church. Christ had called him to oppose a government that trampled all of God's divine mandates.

Along with his brother-in-law and friends, Bonhoeffer became involved in a plot to overthrow Hitler. In a sudden move, Bonhoeffer was arrested and imprisoned in April, 1943, and remained in prison two years. One Sunday after leading a worship service for the prisoners, Bonhoeffer was called out of his cell. As his fellow prisoners gathered to tell him good bye, Bonhoeffer took an English officer aside and told him, "This is the end, but it is the beginning of life."[3]

Six years before Dietrich Bonhoeffer fell into the hands of the Gestapo, he had written, "When Christ calls a man, he bids him come and die." On April 9, 1945—just a few days before Allied Forces arrived—Bonhoeffer was hanged at Flossenburg Prison.

---

3. Dietrich Bonhoeffer's biographical sketch, including his final conversation with the English officer, is found in John W. Doberstein's introduction to Bonhoeffer's *Life Together* (New York: Harper, 1954).

Only God knows the ultimate cost of following Jesus Christ in the arena of government. But I believe there is a *minimum* cost: to work diligently at the tasks of being an obedient citizen and developing a hearing HEART. Like Bonhoeffer, I may hear God call me to a specific witness to the lordship of Christ over all governments. And I may be asked to put my life on the line that a government might protect ordinary people—the ordinary people God cares about and gave his Son that they might have life.

The final reward for following Christ in the arena of government may be to see the gospel of Jesus Christ move freely in my high-tech world. With the proper use of this freedom and with the commitment of ordinary Christians, Christ can come alive in a new way in the families, churches, and workplaces of a world as they are slowly brought under the dominion of Jesus Christ.

14. The Arena of the Church (Gathered)

What is your strategy for going to church?

The first answer that comes to mind is my precisely timed travel schedule, which allows me to arrive at the exact split second required to get a parking space close to the church when the early worship service lets out.

But do I have to come up with a serious answer? Maybe I have finally pushed the strategy issue one step too far! Why should I have to think through a strategy for being involved in my own congregation? Of all the activities in which I am involved as a layman, it seems that nothing should be more spontaneous, natural, and unstructured than my involvement in the life of my own congregation. I need a sanctuary from the world, especially from the high-tech world. And I need corporate worship to praise God. I need teaching and preaching that will equip and encourage me to be obedient to my call to work and ministry in the world.

The Church Gathered can and must give me all of this. The question of strategy comes back into focus when I ask what I will give to the Church Gathered.

STRATEGIES FOR THE LONG HAUL

A number of the most effective lay leaders I've known seem to have quiet strategies that guide their ministries within their congregations. I have never forgotten how irate and frustrated I became years ago with an associate minister who opposed my plans for a singles' class retreat. I ran complaining to the class sponsor, who was a respected elder, corporate executive, and civic leader. He patiently heard me out, then urged me to calm down and to quit worrying. I caught a glimpse of strategy in his comment: "A lot of preachers have come and gone, but I'm still here." His strategy for being effective in his church was to sign on for the long haul.

When talking about strategy, I think it helps to look at church membership the same way we have looked at the other divinely mandated arenas of work, family, and government. More important than our needs for social and business contacts, convenience, and emotional reassurance is the call we have from Jesus Christ to be part of a fellowship of believers. When I hear this call, I can begin to accept the fact that the basic reason I am in church at all is the fact that involvement in church is a divine mandate. (After all, if I loyally showed up at church every time the doors opened for fifty years, and if that is *not* what God wanted me to do, my church attendance would go down in "the book" as sin!)

The beginning of a strategy for lay ministry in the Church Gathered, then, is to see the congregation as a place where God has called me to be. I may come to a particular congregation because it is near my home, because my parents belong, because I like the preaching, or because a friend invited me. But regardless of how I get there, my life in the congregation must eventually be shaped by my obedience to Jesus Christ.

TWO KINDS OF LAY LEADERS

Men and women who have found new life in Jesus Christ and are developing their HEARTs will eventually emerge as leaders and servants in the congregations where God has placed them. What each person's role will be and where he or she will play it is, of course, in God's hands. But the two models for lay leadership in the Church Gathered deserve careful study by all potential leaders in a congregation. In an earlier chapter, I described the role of the "e-Leader," which is patterned after that of the first-century elder. This quiet, discipling leadership role—a one-on-one ministry to family, friends, co-workers, and fellow Christians—is a critical link to effective lay ministry in both the Church Gathered and the Church Scattered. The e-Leader, who uses his or her spiritual gifts to build up the people of God, will play a major role in the church of the high-tech age.

But there is a second kind of leadership that is necessary in a congregation—that which involves what I call "institutional oversight" or taking responsibility for the congregation's institutional life. Because of the church's aura of spiritual activity, it is difficult for some of us to visualize and accept the institutional nature of a congregation. But the fact is that once a group of Christians hires a professional staff, buys or rents land and a building, and selects a governing board, that group of Christians has elected to organize in an *institutional* format. And overseeing the way the Church Gathered functions under such a format is a necessary job to which certain lay leaders, as well as certain members of the ministerial staff, are called.

The task of institutional oversight differs from the direct discipling task of the e-Leader (although it is possible for one person to fill both roles). In order clearly to set this role apart, I have coined the term "E-Leader" (with a capital *E*) to refer to the role of institutional oversight—"running the church." This role is patterned historically after that of the lay elders in John Calvin's church in Geneva. These elders were solid local citizens who were actually approved by the city council to oversee the church, schools, and seminary under Calvin's domain.

The E-leader's tasks require a clear understanding of how the Church Gathered functions as an institution once the gothic spires and the stained glass windows are lifted away and the internal structure of the congregation is laid bare. I believe there are five steps that an E-leader must take to prepare a congregation for effective ministry in the high-tech age. But I believe these tasks are shared by every ordinary member of the congregation who is involved with a church committee, organization, program, board, or project.

A strategy for E-leaders must reflect the true ownership of the congregation and serve as a model for everyone called to service and ministry in the congregation. I used to believe that the church belonged to the people who put the sign in the yard. I assumed it belonged either to the denomination who organized it, the staff who ran it, or the folks who footed the bill for the buildings. But I have grown to understand that the congregation belongs not to any of these people or organizations, but to Jesus Christ, and it is accountable to him. Whatever strategy the E-leaders of a congregation elect to follow in the high-tech age is subject to approval by the Lord of the church.

A FOCUS ON LAY MINISTRY

I would like to suggest five top-priority tasks that can serve as the framework of an E-leader's strategy.

The first task is calling the congregation to focus on the ministry of the laity. An E-Leader must concentrate on helping the ordinary Christians in the church to hear God's call and follow him in the high-tech world.

One of my colleagues in the optics business was in the U.S. Air Force and stationed on Long Island when General Douglas MacArthur was recalled as United Nations Commander in the Korean War. My friend's unit marched in the magnificent ticker-tape parade through the streets of New York, right behind five hundred mounted police.

I asked my friend what impressed him most about the actual parade. It wasn't the appearance of General MacArthur! Aside from being behind five hundred horses, the thing he best remembered was mile after mile of troops marching through the streets of New York.

Miles of marching troops—what an image for the church in the high-tech age! But I'm afraid that if that parade had been planned by today's church, it would have consisted only of General MacArthur seated on the back of a convertible, surrounded by the U.S. Army Band and Chorus, rolling slowly through the Big Apple. Just the leaders—no troops.

The church is only now emerging out of a long era in

which many seminaries and congregations have been functionally illiterate as far as lay ministry is concerned. Clergy and laity alike must be reminded again and again that all members of the body of Christ—not just the church professionals—are ministers, and that spiritual gifts are distributed to every member of the congregation. The challenge of the high-tech age is to get the ordinary Christians into the parade!

The early church had a commissioning service for lay ministry; it was called baptism. When people accepted Jesus as the Christ, they were expected to minister in obedience to him. An important task of the E-Leader must be to keep this expectation alive and weave it into the fabric of the institutional congregation. And a very practical aspect of this task is support and encouragement of the clergy and staff as the congregation deepens its commitment to lay ministry.

How do we know when the church leaders are serious about this task of enabling and encouraging lay ministry? I don't have a checklist to judge progress, but I do have a kind of "comfort zone" regarding lay ministry. I can sense when the pastor or senior minister and staff view the congregation as a community of lay ministers. It is even more apparent to me when the ministerial staff see their role as that of equipping and empowering the laity for ministry and when they actually experience a boost in self-worth from this task. I am encouraged when I see my professional minister forming open, vulnerable friendships with lay members and including them in his primary support groups.

I am in my comfort zone when I hear preaching that focuses on biblical values and enables me to deal with the real issues I face while trying to be obedient to Christ in the world—preaching that helps me to identify with Christ and his ministry in the world and the congregation rather than attempting to resolve world issues before my very eyes.

The single most effective way I know to encourage lay ministry is to have lay men and women minister to one another. Historically, the key to lay ministry is an ordinary Christian sharing with others the shape of his own

204

obedience to Jesus Christ. And whether it takes three minutes or thirty, the spoken evidence of God at work in another Christian's life always moves me deeply.

But this kind of witness is often overlooked in the corporate life of the church. I recently had the opportunity to review the plans of the Worship Committee for a major renewal congress. I saw laid out before me four days of outstanding preaching, teaching, music, and worship—but no witness of the laity! It wasn't hard to get the committee to open up some slots for lay witness once I pointed this out, but the point is that no one had even thought of it.

I believe this underutilization of lay witness in congregational worship can be a serious problem for the church in the high-tech age. As ordinary Christians share their lives in small groups and in ministry in the world, they will experience the reality of God alive in the present. A worship service that ignores God at work in the lives of real people *at that moment* and concentrates exclusively on God at work in history or in the lives of antique hymn writers or "professional" ministers will lose touch with the lay ministers who are the congregation.

ASSIGNMENTS BASED ON GIFTS AND ABILITY

I am always impressed by a congregation that structures its corporate life in such a way as to avoid devouring people in congregational maintenance roles. In fact, I believe the second item in the E-Leader's strategy should be the encouragement of selectivity in assigning and accepting tasks within the congregation. For the ironic truth is that in most churches, if I as a layperson show the least aptitude or inclination toward work within the congregation, I will soon face insurmountable opportunities to fill roles! A peek behind the scenes of a normal congregation reveals a multitude of slots to be filled. Those charged with getting people to fill the slots are, unfortunately, sometimes more concerned with just getting the slot filled than with following God's guidance to find the right person for the slot.

The situation in many churches makes me think of the

story about a senior minister and his associate who had a boat. They would row the same layman out on the lake and let him swim back. Each time they would row out a little farther. One day, the layman just couldn't make it and drowned one hundred yards from shore. The senior minister, overcome with anger and disappointment, jumped to his feet, turned to the associate and screamed, "He would have made a good one!"

This is the old "use 'em up and burn 'em out" approach to lay leadership, and it can be highly detrimental to the church. To avoid it, E-Leaders must work at structuring congregational life around a different model. And this also means that each layperson must assume responsibility for balancing his or her *own* ministry. If we are in the congregation out of obedience to Jesus Christ, any assignment we accept must be accepted out of prayerful obedience to Christ.

The practical issues are balance and stewardship. I must balance my congregational involvement against the three other arenas of ministry. I must also be a steward of my own spiritual gifts. The congregation may roll out a variety of roles for me to play, but I must seek the assignments that will use my spiritual gifts.

The church cannot afford to quench people's gifts for ministry by randomly assigning roles that need filling. It is important for the laity in congregations to spend as little time as possible playing roles and as much time as possible exercising the spiritual gifts God has given them to build up his church.[1]

EXCELLENCE AND ACCOUNTABILITY

I believe the third element in a strategy for an E-Leader should be an insistence on excellence in the operation of the congregation.

In the last few years, there has been a trend toward evaluating and holding accountable those institutions that influ-

---

1. An insightful book on the subject of spiritual gifts and their use is Peter Wagner, *Your Spiritual Gifts* (Ventura, CA: Regal, 1979).

ence and shape our lives. The searchlight has been turned on law, banking, government, education, and medicine. American industry has been recently scrutinized in the bestseller, *In Search of Excellence,* by Thomas J. Peters and Robert H. Waterman, Jr.[2]

But for some unexplained reason, the same lay men and women who demand excellence in other institutions tend to check their critical faculties at the door when they enter the church and are content to accept mediocrity as the norm for congregational life. A great church management myth has appeared which says that mediocre music, teaching, preaching, youth work, and outreach programs are about the best that you can expect from a congregation.

I believe an E-Leader must lead a quest for excellence in the one organization that bears the name of Jesus Christ in the high-tech age. But I don't mean excellence according to the standards of business and industry, which may carry connotations of materialism and cutthroat competition. I am talking about excellence on Christ's terms—running a church according to the highest standards of faithfulness, obedience, and love. By "insisting on excellence," I mean holding myself and each other accountable to develop our HEARTs as God wants us to.

When I have personally pushed for this kind of performance accountability, however, I have encountered resistance from some church bureaucrats and clergy. Part of their defense is rooted in an attempt to hide behind an unrealistic, "totally spiritual" view of the institutional church, which, in their minds, gives it a sort of "diplomatic immunity." They are reluctant to admit that when the church organizes as an institution, it is accountable for its achievements and level of performance in the services and ministries it sponsors.

A second evasive maneuver in congregational management is to invoke an imaginary rule that claims that "business methods" are not applicable and will not work in the church. It *is* true that the church is not a business and should not be run as such. But that is really beside the point. In

---

2. New York: Warner, 1982.

saying that excellence should be a priority, I am not saying congregations should be evaluated against business standards, but should be judged by managerial expertise, professional competence, and performance levels appropriate to the church. The E-Leader must expect excellence in the institutional life of the congregation and hold the people who work there accountable.

As we enter the high-tech age, the institutional church has proven itself highly resistant to self-renewal. E-Leaders, therefore, have the responsibility to continually sift through the activities sponsored by their congregations and seek God's evaluation of the performance. The call to excellence must center on excelling at obedience to Jesus Christ in the corporate life and ministry of the congregation.

THINKING STRATEGICALLY

The fourth task in the E-Leader's strategy is to call the congregation to strategic thinking and planning. Last spring, *Leadership* magazine invited a group of the nation's successful pastors to meet together and to discuss congregational effectiveness. They used the term "fortress churches" to describe stagnant congregations and "entrepreneurial churches" to describe the dynamic, effective ones. An entrepreneur can be defined as "someone who shifts resources from less productive to more productive use." The E-Leader's task is to direct the congregation into entrepreneurial ministry through strategic planning.

I have discovered that congregations tend to be most comfortable with short-range operational planning (for instance, how many staff members and how much money will it take to keep on going for one more year?) or perhaps long-range operational planning (What will be required for the congregation to keep on doing the same thing for the next three-to-five years?).

But there is also a critical need for strategic planning, which asks, "What business are we in?" and "What business *should* we be in as a congregation?" I believe E-Leaders must learn to think and plan strategically in order to guide the church's transition into the high-tech age. And this strategic planning cannot be done by a committee or a single person, but must involve the whole congregation. (A recent cover story in *Business Week* focused on the disastrous results in American business when strategic planning tasks were removed from those who must actually do the work.)

The process of strategic planning requires three distinct steps. As I indicated above, the process begins with the question: What business are we in? This question tends to generate a lot of theological verbiage, which can be largely ignored while a careful study of the operating budget is made to come up with an answer (whatever commands the largest percentage of the budget is almost certainly the church's top priority).

The process moves next to the question: What business *should* we be in? Most congregations will face a major task in defining their call to ministry in the high-tech age. My belief is that this question can only be answered when the E-Leaders bring the congregation together for prayerful creative dreaming where the burdens that are on the HEARTs of the laity can emerge.

When the "what" is identified, the next step is to ask "how" it is to be accomplished. At this point, the professional staff, E-Leaders, and concerned laity can meet to convert the new goals into practical tactics. If the new ministry thrust fits the old program structure, it must be located in the existing organization and encouraged. If it is a true entrepreneurial new venture, it must be nurtured and protected until it sprouts and springs to life.

Each strategic area of ministry must then be reduced to a "bite-sized" program that can be funded and assigned staff and lay team members. E-Leaders as a final step will oversee and review the progress in bringing new directions of ministry to life and terminating those activities that have outlived their usefulness.

A CALL TO RENEWAL

The final task in the personal strategy of an E-Leader is that of calling the congregation to renewal. As a rule, *per-*

sonal renewal is much better understood than *congregational* renewal. Personal renewal means that an individual abandons his or her life to Jesus Christ and gets on with the tasks of developing the HEART and a personal ministry. Congregational renewal can be described as God's doing "a new thing in our time." Some examples would be new forms of worship, music, or ministry.

The key to understanding congregational renewal for the high-tech age is a precise definition of *what* is being renewed. Congregational renewal, at its deepest level, is renewal of the covenant relationship between God and his people. Jeremiah describes such renewal as seen from God's perspective:

> I will set my eyes upon them for good, . . . I will build them up and not tear them down; I will plant them, and not uproot them. I will give them a HEART to know that I am the LORD; and they shall be my people and I will be their God, for they shall return to me with their whole HEART (Jer. 24:6–7).

This Word of God, spoken through Jeremiah, adds the interesting twist that even corporate renewal of the people of God is a matter of the HEART. It is the HEART that must perceive and know the Lord God in the crowd of distractions, idols, and false gods that compete for our attention and imagination.

When God and his people renew their covenant, a dynamic process is set in motion. For a people to return to God, he must *redeem* them from that which holds them captive. The people must *repent,* which is the act of turning loose and turning away from whatever they hold on to instead of the Lord God. God then makes the next move to *restore* his people. The process of congregational renewal flows from redemption to repentence to restoration. It is only after these three steps are taken that God calls for *reform.*

I believe the key to true congregational renewal is keeping this order straight. In Presbyterian congregations, the elders, deacons, and ministerial staff make up the recognized group of E-Leaders. As I have served as an elder, I have noticed we have a dangerous tendency to skip to *reform* and omit the other three steps for congregational renewal. When things are going well and thinking turns to church renewal, reform may consist of implementing a few new programs or just "fixing" a few church problems in the name of renewal. The tendency of an ongoing institution is to keep on rolling down the same track, making a few changes but avoiding the risk of corporate redemption, repentance, or restoration.

This, in my opinion, is nothing less than trying to second-guess God! We must not confuse a few renewal projects even effective ones—with authentic congregational renewal in preparation for a fresh thrust of lay ministry in the high-tech age. As a community, we must come to God and pray to be redeemed from the habits and lifestyles that keep us ineffective as the body of Christ. We must be willing to repent and turn away if necessary from things we hold dear in program and practice. Our hands may have to be empty in order to pick up the new directions for ministry that God will give us.

The step of allowing God to restore us to a position of strength, health, and effectiveness as the body of Christ may be the most difficult step of all because we must accept this restoration as a gift of grace, a kind of corporate "justification by faith." When we have "done everything by the book" as a congregation and have been relatively successful, it is very easy to think that all we need is a little reform. But this is little more than congregational self-justification. Instead, the E-Leaders in a congregation must be prepared to fall at Christ's feet and ask, "Lord, what would you have us do?" Then the entire process of renewal can begin in the preparation for the congregation's mission and ministry to a high-tech world.

As I have given talks on the subject of renewal in the church, one question often comes up: Is there actually hope that the congregation will get its act together in time to survive the high-tech age? I can't second-guess God, of course, but I am able to answer "Yes." Yes, if the ordinary Christians in a congregation are about the disciplines of developing the interior HEART. Yes, if the e-Leaders emerge and lead the troops in discipleship and ministry in the world where they live. Yes, if the E-Leaders of the congregation, the clergy, and the laity together commit their intellects, emotions, ethics, wills, and spiritual lives to see that the institutional life of the congregation is obedient to Jesus Christ.

There is always hope when the people of God come to him with their whole HEARTs.

15. Clusters—A Laboratory for the HEART

The church holds the power and resources to transform the human HEART, even in the high-tech age. What I have called an interior strategy in part 2 of this book is a sketch of the biblical route for developing the HEART to maturity in all five dimensions. When I give my HEART to Jesus, he calls me to step into this stretching, demanding process of spiritual, intellectual, emotional, ethical, and volitional growth. I believe this is the way of a disciple in the high-tech age.

Because I believe that ordinary Christians will be called by God to play a vastly expanded role in the church for the high-tech age, I also believe that each layperson must develop a personal exterior strategy in order to clearly focus on the four arenas of life where Christ calls us to follow him. By working carefully through the call to lay ministry in arenas of work, marriage, government, and the church (both the Church Gathered and the Church Scattered), I have closed the circle of the *laos,* the root word of laity, which in the original Greek usage refers to the whole people of God. The call from Christ to develop the HEART and minister in his name is a call to the *laos*—the partnership of laity and clergy as the whole people of God.

I have tried, without any apology, to view this challenge to the church from a lay perspective. This means both the interior strategy and the exterior strategy that I describe must be effective and practical for everyday living. And the final question from a lay perspective is: Will it work? Can I actually develop my HEART and become effective in ministry and service as I follow Jesus Christ into the high-tech age?

I have personally bet my life on the way of the HEART, and I stand behind this formula I have described in the previous chapters. But there is something still missing. The formula is like my friend Carol Nelson's cookie recipe, which originally came from her grandmother. As a child, Carol loved these cookies, and when she set up housekeeping on her own, she asked her grandmother for the recipe. Well, Carol is a great cook, especially at baking, but her cookies never tasted quite as good as grandma's. Years passed, and Carol finally mentioned this problem to her grandmother, who finally admitted that she had left a few ingredients out of the recipe.

As far as I know, her grandma never did tell Carol what was missing. But in this chapter I want to focus in on the missing element—to make the recipe complete.

A PLACE TO GROW

The missing ingredient is a place dedicated to the development of the HEART—a laboratory where I can formulate my strategy for lay ministry. I need a place where I can risk being Christ's person and still be safe from the hostile environment of the high-tech world.

I also need people who are partners in this adventure of the HEART, and partners in a call to lay ministry and service. Like J. R. R. Tolkien's fictional hobbits, who like their meals "regularly and often," I need these partners regularly and often.

I could describe my group of partners of the HEART as a small group, which it is, or as a Christian fellowship, which it also is. Because I have in mind a very special kind of small-group fellowship, I will call it by a special name—a cluster, which can be described as a number of similar things growing together.

The people in a cluster are similar in their commitment to follow Jesus Christ in ministry to the world. They are similar in their desire to develop their HEARTs through corporate worship and study, as well as through the practice

214

of the personal disciplines of the interior HEART. They are similar in that their HEARTs are being tested daily as they move out into the four arenas of life.

The people of a cluster must be open to growing together. This means each person in the cluster must accept the need for confrontation, affirmation, and vulnerability—these three things added together make up the equation for growth. If I refuse to be vulnerable and instead protect myself by hiding my true self, my growth will be stunted. If I am too fearful and oversensitive to confront or be confronted, I will stagnate. Without affirmation, I have no encouragement to grow or to encourage others to see their potential as they put their lives in God's hands.

CLUSTERS AREN'T OPTIONAL!

Over the last twenty-five years, small-group insights from modern psychology have been translated in practical, helpful ways for the church. Writers such as Bruce Larson, Keith Miller, and Paul Tournier have introduced many of us to a healthy merger of psychological and theological truth. Now I believe the time has come when the laity *must* form clusters if there is to be an effective strategy for the church in the high-tech age. Without effective, functioning clusters that offer support and encouragement, the chances of success are drastically lowered for ordinary Christians who are attempting to develop the HEART and minister in the hostile, negative environment of the high-tech world.

A cluster is the place where the Church Scattered finds common ground with the Church Gathered. I have seen clusters bring new life and growth to longtime members in the congregation. I have also seen Christ come alive in a cluster out in some pocket of the world and bring amazing spiritual vitality where it was least expected.

CLUSTERS IN MY LIFE

Becoming aware of the power of clusters has been a gradual process for me. When I entered graduate school at the University of Washington, the hippie era was starting to crest. I lived on the floor of a dormitory reserved for graduate students, which was as close to a spiritual vacuum as I care to get.

During the winter quarter, the floor president, a man who had dropped out of a Catholic seminary after seven years, came in to ask a favor. Dick said that his priest told him, "The reason the Protestants love Christ more than we do is because we don't know anything about him." He asked if I would help him study the Bible.

We picked up eight other students on our floor who wanted to go through the Gospel of John with us. I will never forget asking two roommates if they were interested in coming to the Bible study. They just looked at each other and said, "We are atheists . . . but we sure don't know anything about the Bible. Sure, we'll come." I realized later that they had never even been in a church, so they just *assumed* that they were atheists because they didn't know anything about Christianity.

A few months later, I was introduced to Ad Sewell, the lay ministry coordinator at University Presbyterian Church on the edge of the campus. Upon learning that I was from Oklahoma and Texas, he quickly asked if I knew Keith Miller, had ever been to Laity Lodge, or had ever been in a small group. I answered, "Yes," to all of the above.

Ad pointed to his desk drawer and said that he had five hundred names of people who had indicated they wanted to be in small groups. He asked what I thought they ought to do about it.

I gave the first answer that popped into my head: "Start one group." So, in a few weeks, I saw my first cluster take shape in a congregation. Six of us formed a 6:30 A.M. men's group in Seattle. I was surprised to see members of the congregation realize that they could be themselves and still be loved and accepted. When this soaked in, their HEARTs came alive and began to develop right in the congregational setting.

A LIFE-CHANGING CLUSTER

In recent years, my most dramatic experience of the power of a cluster within the arena of the Church Gathered began when I met Bobby Bridewell.[1] Bobby was working with the wealthiest investors in Dallas buying, selling, and developing hotel properties. I was invited to lunch by Bobby and three of his friends. They wanted to start a study group of some kind and had gotten my name from the director of counseling at our church.

The idea of a group had started several weeks earlier when Bobby had called his friend, Boots, and wanted to meet for a drink after work. As they talked in the bar, Bobby explained that he felt something was missing in his life. He didn't know if it was God or Christ or what. And he had come to Boots because Boots was the only person he could think of who might help but wouldn't put a religious hard sell on him.

Boots had been in a group once that worked on questions like Bobby's. So together they decided to start such a group. By the time we met for our lunch at the country club, they had picked up a doctor and two lawyers from our church who wanted to get in on whatever we decided to do.

I signed on as their leader. Each week, we met at the urologist's office to eat lunch and to read and discuss a chapter from the Gospel of Luke. Each person, including Bobby and a lawyer who was also there as a "seeker," took a turn reading the chapter and a layman's commentary ahead of time and leading the discussion.

Bobby spontaneously made up ground rules as we went along. One day he announced, "Now, fellows, I've been a millionaire. I also lost it all and have been broke. I've started over and built my business back. Whatever it is I'm looking for, that isn't it. I've been married with a lovely family and home. I lost it in a divorce and started over with a new family. That isn't it either."

A few weeks later, out of the clear blue sky, he reported, "Fellows, we are never going to figure this thing out using just our heads. We are going to have to use our HEARTs." For nearly forty years, Bobby Bridewell had lived on a fast track and refused to accept the Texas Bible-Belt guidelines

---

1. Several years ago, Bobby requested that I use every opportunity to tell the story of his spiritual journey. He was deeply concerned that others know what had happened to him through his encounter with God.

for living his life. Now he was feeling a firm but gentle nudge from the spiritual dimension of his HEART, that was waiting to be exercised and developed.

Bobby still could not name what he was looking for, but he began to exercise his HEART with prayer, Bible study, and serious questioning. I fought the temptation to tell him how to clean up his act with a list of some of my personal spiritual values. Instead, I waited and watched as the desire to make contact with true spiritual reality grew stronger. The need of his HEART to make contact with God came into sharper focus for Bobby, and he refused to let this issue be clouded over by business pursuits, family and social life, or even religious activities.

We continued to meet for several months. One week, our regular meeting fell on the day that Bobby was in the hospital for a routine physical exam. We met at the scheduled time but in his hospital room. The next day one of the group called me with unbelievable news. The physical exam had turned up cancer of the lymph system, and Bobby was still in the hospital.

I forced myself to trudge back to the hospital a day later to face Bobby and his unexpected tragic news. When I arrived, he was alone at the table in a large suite reading a newspaper. We fumbled for a few moments with nervous small talk.

Bobby finally smiled and said, "Well, yesterday was the greatest day of my life. When they told me I had cancer early in the morning, I spent half a day with the normal fears and worries and terror everyone goes through. Then, along about noon, something happened. I realized I wasn't afraid to die. Slocum, it all worked! Everything you and the boys told me and all I've read in Luke is real for me. Christ has become real for me and is in this with me!"

Bobby was grateful to God that he had been allowed to work on his spiritual quest before he got the news about his cancer, because he thought he was so hardheaded and strong-willed that he would never have turned to God just because he was ill. Now, however, contact with God energized the spiritual dimension of his HEART, and a new life opened up for him. Even though the doctors were optimistic that the cancer could be arrested with chemotherapy, Bobby knew that his life expectancy was shortened. So the challenge to develop his HEART and share his discovery with his friends and family became a top priority.

Our cluster continued to meet, and we worshiped together on Sunday and attended the same Sunday school class. Bobby began therapy, and his urgency about developing his HEART, as well as his gratitude to God for life itself, touched us all. Bobby wanted a second cluster, so he could invite longtime friends he cared about and share what he had found.

CLUSTERS AMONG THE CHURCH SCATTERED

Bobby and Hugh, the lawyer who was also a seeker, found Christ through our cluster, and the changes in their lives sent waves rippling throughout the church and community. But what, if anything, can clusters do in the arenas of the Church Scattered—beyond the protected shelter of the Church Gathered? Try the physics department of the University of Texas at Austin as a tough place to experiment with clusters. When I was in graduate school there, I realized that my weird and wonderful friends of this international scientific community had very real needs for spiritual and emotional development. So I set out to see how open they were and to discover a way to reach out to them.

I had met a bright young graduate student from Groesbeck, Texas, during my first semester in Austin. Preston was riding high on a new-found faith in Christ, so it wasn't hard to hook him on the question: What does it mean to be Christ's person in the physics department? Night after night as we studied together, an entrepreneurial idea was taking shape. Why not start a Bible study in the physics department?

Preston and I reserved an impressive conference room in the new wing for noon on Thursdays. We personally invited both our American and international friends. A dozen or so showed up and we began a study of the Gospel of John.

I'm afraid that if our entrepreneurial venture had been in the business arena, we would have filed for bankruptcy. It was a disaster. The academic setting did us in. We kept our discussions on an impersonal, intellectual level, and our reserved and reluctant guests drifted away one by one. We committed the dreaded mistake of boring everyone—including ourselves—with the Gospel, because we never got personal.

The group eventually disbanded with a silent sigh of relief. At least we learned that technical experts don't like to be theological novices.

With this ministry experiment in the high-tech academic arena behind me, I was free to focus my total attention on grabbing the gold ring—a doctorate in physics. I had just a few months left to prepare for the two-day exam that would decide if I was to be admitted to the doctoral program. Only two out of three applicants would qualify. I learned right then and there that I could be motivated by raw fear of failure.

I felt the pressure build as I hit the summer months of around-the-clock study. I shared an office with a straight-"A" graduate student named Roger. We studied and reviewed together, and as the exam date got closer, my raw, competitive edges began to show. I picked up momentum and hit the forty-eight hours of examinations like a runaway train. Suddenly, it was over and, a week later, word came that the names of those who passed were posted. My heart stopped as my eyes scanned down the list to "Slocum, Robt. E." I had made it!

But something was wrong! I scanned the list again for Roger's name. It was missing. My office partner hadn't made it. I was sorry for him, although I knew that, with his straight-"A" record, he would get another chance the next year if he wanted to try. In the remaining weeks of summer, I saw Roger struggle silently with the decision of whether to stay in Austin and try again or take his wife and children back to his old job in Florida. As far as I knew, he had never failed at anything he had ever tried before.

I waited and watched, not knowing what to say or do. All I could get out was, "Roger, God has meant a lot to me in the high places as well as the low. Here is something [a booklet] you might want to look at. It helped me figure out God's plan for my life." He did not respond.

A few days later, an old friend from Oklahoma came by our office. He was starting graduate school in psychology, and I introduced Keith to Roger. Before I knew it, Roger had actually shared his bitter disappointment over the failed exam and his frustration about the future. Then I opened up for the first time with Roger about being forced out of the University of Washington by poor grades. Keith and I both made the point that God specializes in new starts, and that as we had worked through down-and-out experiences, we had found that the Christ we had asked to manage our lives was a tremendous source of hope. Roger finally looked at us and said, "You know, this really is interesting. I'd like to get together with you and talk some more."

We agreed to bring a sack lunch and meet there in the office at noon the following Wednesday. As an afterthought, we agreed that anyone else we thought might want to sit in should be invited. If they asked what we were going to do, we would tell them we were going to talk about how to survive in graduate school.

When lunchtime rolled around that Wednesday, nearly two dozen people, holding sack lunches, lined the walls of our small office. While we ate, each person told who he was and spoke of his hopes and obstacles for the coming semester.

The warmth of that circle of men and women felt like a port in a growing storm. But we knew that, with this crowd, we'd have to find a new place to meet! My experiments were being set up in an isolated lab in the second basement of the physics building, so I suggested we go there. The catacombs I had visited in Rome were no darker or mustier than the light-tight lab where our new group of seekers and strugglers would meet each week for the next year and a half. We were the "catacombs" cluster from that point on.

221

Our dozen or so regulars included chemists, mathematicians, physicists, psychologists, biologists, engineers, and an English major.

We had no structured plan for the noon meeting, but an agenda emerged. We had gathered around the very real issue of survival—both professional and personal—in graduate school. Some of us had no personal faith or deep religious convictions. As we ate our sack lunches, each person took a turn and told about the struggles and victories of the past week and described what was coming down the track toward them in the week ahead. We reported on exams passed or failed, research successes and failures, the pains and pressures of academic politics, and the professors who held our futures in the palms of their hands.

Next, we went around the circle a second time. This happened spontaneously as those of us who were attempting to open our lives to Christ described the difference it made to have God as a part of these experiences. Those who had never been exposed to this kind of personal faith were seeing God at work in human lives.

As we described our experiments of faith, they were able to read our lives like a laboratory notebook. We all found care, love, and support in the brown bag lunch crew. It was also a place of honest spontaneous witness to resources that could be tapped by prayer, Scripture study, and books. These resources allowed God to become real in this intellectual fortress where we were all voluntarily imprisoned.

In Rome during the early Christian era, the catacombs were used as a refuge for men and women who put their lives on the line to follow Jesus, the Christ. The world of everyday Rome had become so hostile and difficult for them that they met in the catacombs for worship and sharing, and to care for and support one another in hard times. In the catacombs in Austin, God became real and HEARTs began to grow. One by one, each person in the cluster who had come without a personal relationship with Christ opened their lives to him.

My firsthand experience with the growth and ministry that comes out of clusters has convinced me that networks of clusters, both in the Church Gathered and Church Scattered, are the keys to effective lay ministry in the high-tech age. Ordinary Christians must have a regular place to identify and clarify what Christ calls them to do and be. We need to be regularly empowered and commissioned for ministry by people who know and love us. We need the support of people to whom we can tell our stories and who will listen and care. We need people who will hold us accountable for the development of our HEARTs and for responsible obedience to Jesus Christ in the arenas of our lives. The cluster can provide that kind of love and support and accountability in the catacombs of the high-tech age.

Epilogue:

The Focus

This book grew out of an idea that began ten years ago—my "Project HEART." Initially, I responded to Michael Maccoby's description of an "underdeveloped heart" in high-technology managers by giving a set of informal talks and leading small-group studies. This material was first pulled together in a manuscript aimed at high-tech people living in an ordinary world. I set the manuscript aside to make a detailed study of the biblical concept of the HEART. And as I began to grasp the resources God provides for the HEART, my concept of my audience changed. I was interested in reaching not only high-tech people in an ordinary world, but also ordinary people in a high-tech world.

As a layman with a family and a business, I realize one very definite paradox in the material found in parts 2 and 3. The paradox is that I feel the tug of Christ's call to develop my HEART and serve in the arenas of work, government, marriage, and the church, but I have only a limited amount of time. Where will the time come from?

For a lay man or woman who seriously wants to be Christ's person in the high-tech age, the stress and tension can be hard to handle. How do I balance my role as a discipling e-Leader in the world with my role as E-Leader providing institutional oversight for the congregation? (You can't be in two meetings at once!) How do I balance my commitment to the Church Gathered with my commitment to ministry in the Church Scattered? How do I divide my time between my wife and family and my daily work? How do I tell when God calls me to step away from all of this to make time to serve the community as a whole?

This is the paradox. I must be obedient to Christ's call, but there is no way I can do everything! The high-tech age only complicates the matter by speeding up life until it becomes a blur.

THE KEY TO THE BALANCING ACT

The only answer I can offer is that an ordinary Christian in the high-tech age must accept this problem of too little time and too much to do and realize it will never go away. This is the dilemma of the laity. Our lives are not partitioned off in neat cells like the rooms and daily schedule of the monastery.

But I do believe there is one key to balancing life, even in the high-tech age. That key is what I call "the focus."

The focus is found in the prologue to 1 John under the heading (in the New English Bible), "Recall to Fundamentals":

> It was there from the beginning; we have heard it; we have seen it with our own eyes; we looked upon it, and felt it with our own hands; and it is of this we tell. Our theme is the word of life. This life was made visible; we have seen it and bear our testimony; we here declare to you the eternal life which dwelt with the Father and was made visible to us. What we have seen and heard we declare to you, so that you and we together may *share in a common life,* that life which we share with the Father and his Son Jesus Christ. And we write this in order that the joy of us all may be complete (1 John 1:1–4, NEB).

John, the disciple closest to Jesus, focuses on the fact that I share in Christ's life and Christ shares in my life. And because you and I both share a common life with Christ, we share a common life with each other. This *common shared* life is the focus of the entire Christian enterprise. (I much prefer the translation, "share in a common life" to the more well-known translation—"have fellowship," because it helps me grasp the full scope of the prologue. "Fellowship" to me has meant pot luck church suppers and playing Ping-Pong at the church on Sunday night!)

I am convinced that the common shared life with Christ and members of his body, the church, is also the key to balanced lay ministry in the high-tech age. Christ must walk through my life with me and day-by-day guide me in the development of my HEART and in my involvement in the arenas of work, church, government, and family.

Nearly thirty years ago, Dr. Robert Munger delivered a sermon on this subject one Sunday evening in Berkeley, California. The sermon became the booklet, *My Heart, Christ's Home,* and millions of copies have been distributed. The appeal of the booklet is the down-to-earth picture it gives of the human HEART as a home where Christ knocks on the door. The excited but jittery host then leads the Lord on a tour of the rooms of his life. The drama unfolds as the owner of the house struggles to decide what to do with this royal guest wandering around in the interior of his life.

The conclusion of Dr. Munger's sermon leads back to the focus of John's prologue: Christ cannot put the house in order and give balance to the life until the owner turns the deed of ownership over to Christ. My hope for a balanced, ordered life and ministry in the high-tech age lies in Christ's ability to order my life when I abandon each dimension of my HEART and each arena of my life to him.

A FAMILY ROOM FOR THE HEART

A few years ago, Dr. Munger was asked in an interview what, if anything, he would change if he could write his booklet over. He explained that the story described a one-on-one meeting of Christ and an individual, and that the story worked through the issue of sanctification, the process of setting each area of life apart for God's use. He said that his only change would be to build on one additional room—a family room—to his "home." In the intervening years Dr. Munger had come to a new appreciation of the importance of the brothers' and sisters' in Christ's family getting together.

I've never seen any one with a better, natural appreciation for the family getting together than my friend, Bobby Bridewell, whose story I started in the last chapter. Bobby's cancer was put into remission, and his instinctive love for people caused him to get with all the people he knew and cared about to encourage them and share his new-found life in Christ. Then, one afternoon, I called his house and was asked to hurry over.

Bobby had just returned from the doctor's office, and the doctor had told him the cancer was terminal. He had, at the most, months to live. But Bobby said he planned to live those few months to the fullest and to take life one day at a time with Jesus Christ. He had called me over to pray together and to invite me to go with him down the path leading to his physical death. I agreed, but I wondered how in the world God could get me through this walk with my friend, who had just turned forty.

Our original cluster—Bill, Boots, Don, Hugh, and I—met with Bobby every Saturday for prayer and Scripture study. We were experiencing a common shared death at the human level, but each week we kept going with the knowledge that our common shared life with Christ was eternal.

Bobby had unusually high tolerance for pain, and during those months his mind stayed clear. His ministry never stopped, and friend after friend came to comfort him and went away comforted. I sat in the corner of his hospital room one afternoon while Bobby visited with two former business associates. I witnessed a very strange example of bedside manner when one "friend," who had said that he and Bobby used to "sweep out bars together," finally asked, "Bobby, what the hell went through your mind when they told you that you had cancer?"

Bobby smiled and patted his Bible. "The Book, the promises in the Book, fellows. You probably didn't know that I found Christ before I got the cancer, and my family and I are well taken care of. I've had a great life, met a lot of wonderful people, and been a lot of places. And I'm doing great, just great."

THE FOCUS

A FINAL WORD

When Bobby finally grew too weak for visits from the entire cluster group, I went to the hospital alone each Saturday. We would always swap entrepreneurial "war stories" and talk about Bobby's race horses, then pray and open the Scriptures.

Early one week, Bobby called in our senior minister to discuss specific requests for his funeral service. The following Saturday morning he and I visited a few moments and read Psalm 23. That night he was gone.

Our church, the largest Presbyterian church in Dallas, was packed for the funeral. In the funeral service, Dr. Bell faithfully delivered Bobby's message to his friends and family: "Tell them Christ was with me every step of the way."

Bobby had a deep appreciation for the fact that not only had God given us the gift of himself in Jesus Christ, but he has given us the gift of each other. The focus of the church for the age of high technology is still a common shared life with Jesus Christ and all who follow him.

Bobby put into words what I believe is the final guideline for the ordinary Christians—lay men and women—who respond to Christ's call to develop the HEART and move out to be his people in the high-tech world. As I move up the mountain and gaze up at the peak, searching for the courage to take the next step God wants me to take, I must know one thing:

Christ is with us every step of the way.

Acknowledgments

This book is the result of an informal personal project in lay ministry that evolved in bits and pieces over the last ten years. Many people have played a part in Project HEART, and I want to thank them for their contributions to the project, to the manuscript, and to me.

I am grateful to Bruce Larson and to the elders of the University Presbyterian Church in Seattle for a delightful weekend at the base of Mt. Rainier and the opportunity to present part 3 of this book in a series of messages at their annual retreat. Dr. Ernie Lewis, Rev. Robert Henderson, Bill Yinger, Dr. B. Clayton Bell—all partners in planning the 1985 Presbyterian Congress on Renewal—have urged me to make a strong case for lay ministry and made it possible for me to present part 1 as a Congress workshop. My thanks go out to Howard Butt, Jr., and Howard Hovde for the opportunity to teach the development of the HEART at the summer Contemplative Week at Laity Lodge.

I owe additional thanks to Clayton Bell and the Highland Park Presbyterian Church community for continuing encouragement of my own lay ministry and for the opportunity to refine this material in the Omnibus series and numerous church school classes. I am grateful to Dr. Michael Maccoby, director of the Project on Work, Technology, and Character, who made time for an interview and review of portions of the manuscript.

Without the help of many of my partners in lay ministry who encouraged me and read manuscripts at various stages of development, the project would have died. I am grateful to Ed Dittrich, John Aust, Sam Rodehaver, Billie Slocum Jones, Howard Blake, Mark Gibbs, Bob David, and Bill and Faye Sarjeant for their opinions and suggestions. Roger and Jeannie Bryant thought of the idea of a grant and provided major funding, along with significant help from Bruce and Jan Harbour and Billie Slocum Jones. My thanks to them and to Creath Davis and the Christian Concern Foundation for administering the grant for research on the biblical concept of the HEART.

I must thank Howard Blake and Bill Cody for their indirect contribution to the book as my teachers of lay ministry. Laity Lodge has been my "home base" for lay studies since its founding, and I am grateful to Bill Cody for the many times he served as my host, pastor, and teacher. Howard Blake has served as my mentor and has shown me lay ministry in a global perspective as we have served together in "The Laity—A New Direction" fellowship.

I want to thank several people who simply cheered and prayed. This group includes Fred Browning; Linda's Monday morning prayer group; and Paul Williams and the "Austin Group." Thanks for being there.

To the three pastors who originally pointed me to the mountain and took me there—Otto Bergner, C. Ralston Smith, and Jim Craddock—I am thankful to you for life in Christ.

My words of appreciation go to those who have helped produce the actual manuscripts. Bob David, Creath Davis, and Ford Madison gave me the use of their personal secretaries for various phases of manuscript preparation. I am grateful for the secretarial help of Debbie Baughan and Carolyn Wright. The major burden fell to Rosie Anthony, who volunteered to lead a heroic charge on the publication deadline and meet the goal.

Anne Christian Buchanan of Word Publishing accepted the task of transforming my manuscript from a lengthy technical memo into a book that could actually be read by ordinary people. I am grateful for her editorial skill, insight, enthusiasm for the book and—last but not least—her belief that there are people out there who truly want renewal to happen.

Keith Miller, who introduced me to lay ministry twenty-five years ago, maintained confidence in this project and provided practical editorial help and encouragement to keep me from giving up when the fact that I was not a writer caught up with me. Keith's enthusiasm for the project rubbed off on Doc Heatherley and Ernie Owen of Word, Inc., and I am grateful to them for mapping the route to get these words into print.

I owe my wife, Linda, a debt which I can never repay for her many, many contributions as a resident editor who has never failed to believe in what I am doing. She has personally sacrificed and suffered for Christ in order that this book could be written.

A final word to my son, Paul: I apologize for the fishing trips we missed and all the delays in your electronics projects because I was too busy to take you to Radio Shack.

And to all who have been partners in our journey to the summit, including those whose names I have failed to mention, I thank you and thank God that we have been on the journey together.

A Guide for Discussion and Reflection

Since the focus of this book is the role of ordinary Christians—the laity—in the church and the world it is my hope that some of you may want to work on your personal strategy for lay ministry by studying and discussing the book together. To help with this, I have prepared a group of questions for each chapter; these can be used by a class, a study group, a discussion group, or a share-and-support group. You may also find them a useful aid to individual reflection (consider yourself a group of one). Several questions reflecting on relevant biblical passages have been included for those wanting to focus on topical Bible study.

Although I have made a point of writing specifically for lay men and women, it would be a great idea to use these questions as a basis for dialogue between clergy and laity on the subject of lay ministry and the role of the laity in your own congregation.

The questions are not "tests" on the theories and ideas presented in the chapters. There are no yes/no or true/false questions. What you will find are questions about practical relationships in your life. The questions have the flavor of asking, "How does it work for you?"

HOW TO USE THIS GUIDE IN A GROUP

When I am asked how to start a group, I have a simple answer: Find one other person who is interested in what you want to do. Once the two of you agree to the group, you can ask God to bring along anyone else who should be in the group. You may be surprised at who turns up. But no matter what, you and your partner will be on your way.

I would suggest that each group member read the chapter in advance. You may each want to get a special notebook to use for recording questions, comments, prayer requests, and any special word that comes to you from the Lord as you read and look over the questions prior to the actual group time.

The group may decide to have a regular leader, or leadership may rotate among group members. To encourage participation by all in the group, I like, at least at the start, to go around the circle and let each person give his or her answer. I have found that it is helpful for the leader to go first and model the answer. (But if the leader gives impersonal or superficial answers, the group should let him know. Why waste your time on a discussion that never reaches the level where people really live?)

WHAT ABOUT PRAYER?

If Christ is present whenever two or three are gathered in his name, it might be a good idea for everyone to spend time with him during the group meeting. I like to close a group by allowing each person to voice a prayer. However, since some people are more comfortable praying "out loud" than others, it should be clear that simply saying, "Thank you, God!" is enough.

Sometimes the prayer can focus on a review of personal needs of the people in the group. Another approach may be to review the issues and needs that surfaced during the group discussion and focus prayers of petition on these. You may want to consider at the start of the group a prayer covenant in which each group member agrees to pray daily for every other person in the group by name.

PURPOSE OF DISCUSSION

In chapter 15, I described a special kind of group that I call a cluster (a group of similar things growing together). You may want to scan this chapter in advance to see how a group like this can work.

The goal of a group, I believe, is to find partners for venturing into the high-tech world as followers of Jesus Christ. The group can serve as the base camp for making the climb that God calls you to. It can be a supportive launching place for your enriched lay ministry, as you develop your personal strategy for following Jesus Christ into the high-tech age.

One Sunday morning, as I taught my adult class, I noticed a sign someone had placed on the wall during the week. It reflected an idea that has been a central theme in every successful group I have been involved with: "If you can't say something spiritual, at least say something honest."

I would like this statement—this theme—to be my final gift to you as your study of the book begins.

Session 1: The Climbing Team
(Preface and Prologue)

In these opening pages, I begin to focus on issues of personal renewal, congregational renewal, and renewal of society and its institutions. I hope to encourage teams of people to come together in order to consider what it means to face these issues and follow Christ in this age of high technology.

I suspect very few people will have the luxury of exploring these questions under the ideal conditions of a roaring fire in Paradise Lodge on the mile-high ridge of Mt. Rainier. As you meet in the ordinary arenas of home, business, or church, I would give you the gift of being a team which somehow can capture the risky excitement of being on this venture together for a short while. New hope for renewal can come alive when you're on such a team.

A team must draw on its members' personal histories, past experiences, and individual gifts and aptitudes, as well as on their shared dream of what it means to achieve the goal of discipleship in a high-tech age. The questions that follow are designed to bring these things to the surface. Each member should be allowed time to reflect on these questions and respond to the group. There are no right or wrong answers, and it is always permissible for an individual to "pass" on a particular question.

1. Using the mountain-climbing image described in chapter 1 (or your own image), describe where you are in your own spiritual pilgrimage at this moment in your life and how it feels.
2. In what ways do you think following Jesus Christ today differs from discipleship in past ages? In what ways are the tasks the same?
3. Read Matthew 8:5–27 silently. After reflection on this passage, describe which of these four models of discipleship best applies to your life today: the centurion (vv. 5–13), Peter's mother-in-law (vv. 14–17), the curious scribe (vv. 18–22), the disciples at sea in the storm (vv. 23–27).
4. As this study begins, do you have some idea of the next step God may call you to take in your own spiritual pilgrimage?
5. In what ways can this group help you understand this next step, find the courage to take it, and develop a strategy to successfully complete the step? (Try to be specific.)

Session 2: The High-Tech Age
(Chapter 1)

The discussion found in chapter 1 underscores the point that the church faces unique challenges in the high-tech age. I believe that the laity must understand and clearly articulate the impact of the high-tech age on individual lives (their own) and lead the church to develop an effective response. Until the problems are defined, it will not be possible to determine if a particular congregation is in a position to respond effectively. The following questions should help the group identify some of the problems and challenges faced by ordinary Christians in a high-tech world.

1. Share with the group examples of ways the high-tech tidal wave has touched your work or lifestyle in a positive way and in a negative way. In general, how do you react to this advance of high-tech technology?

2. Would you characterize your own congregation as First Wave (agricultural village), Second Wave (industrial-type community divided into producers and consumers of religious services), Third Wave (participation by laity in ministry)—or a mixture? Explain your reasons.

3. The church may be required to find a new structure to minister effectively in the high-tech age. As a group, use the following six guidelines to help you develop a creative dream of such a restructured church. Begin by studying the list silently. Then try to come up with some ways a church could carry out some of these guidelines. (At this point, don't worry about being "practical"; open your mind and your imagination!)

    a. Decentralized rather than centralized
    b. Optimum size for effective ministry
    c. Power and decision making distributed among members
    d. Total flexibility as to time and place of ministry
    e. Focus on lay ministry teams over specialized professionals
    f. Diversity in worship, ministry, preaching, and mission in order to customize outreach

4. If the implementation of this creative dream for the church were suddenly up to you, what specific task has the greatest appeal to you personally? What role would you personally play?

5. Much of the apostle Paul's ministry was "on the road" out in the confusing world and away from formal religion and set plans for ministry and service. Read Acts 16 silently, looking for characteristics of Paul's ministry that may fit our efforts to serve Christ in the high-tech age. Go around the group and have each person share one discovery from the passage and tell how it applies to his or her life today.

Session 3: The Church
(Chapter 2)

Evaluation of your own congregation can be a difficult and sometimes emotional task. Some people are quite pleased with their congregation or the pastor and staff and therefore find it difficult to see the congregation's weak areas when it comes to lay ministry. Others are so frustrated with the inadequacies of their congregation that they have trouble seeing its strong points. The following questions are intended to help you focus on your congregation's effectiveness in enabling lay ministry in the various arenas of the high-tech world.

1. Describe *your* response (step by step) to a friend's request to "show me your church!"

2. Go around the circle and have as many people as possible describe from a personal experience an example of each of the following (it might be a good idea just to describe, not name, the congregation):
   a. A caretaker congregation
   b. A "toe-in-the-water" congregation
   c. A congregation with staff-centered renewal ministry
   d. A congregation with lay-ministry-centered renewal
3. How would you describe your own congregation (a, b, c, or d)? Why?
4. What, in your opinion, is the most serious threat to the church in the high-tech age? Explain your answers.
5. What could cause a congregation that fails to equip its lay men and women for ministry in the high-tech world actually to go out of business? (Try to give a specific scenario.)
6. Jesus built his ministry by calling, equipping, and deploying laypeople in God's service. Read Mark 5:35–6:14 and 6:30–32. In these passages, you will find six elements of the discipling process used by Jesus to transform disciples into apostles. They are listed below. Find an example or examples of each element in this passage. What form could this element take in your congregation today?
   a. Modeling
   b. Teaching
   c. Delegating authority
   d. Team ministry
   e. Support groups
   f. Retreat
7. Which of the above list of elements in the discipleship process would best enable and equip you personally for your own service and ministry in the high-tech world? (For example, you may feel the need for Christian role models or a really effective support group.)

Session 4: Inward Strategy
(Chapter 3)

A starting point for developing a personal inward strategy is taking an inventory of the HEART. But because the biblical concept of the HEART may be an unfamiliar concept, it may be difficult to realize that our HEARTs are totally transparent to God. The challenge is to understand the level of development and maturity of our own HEARTs at the present moment and to seek to grow from there.

1. The Psalmist prays, "Search me, O God, and know my HEART." Consider each of the five dimensions and go around the group so each member can share ideas of what it is God is examining in re-

sponse to this prayer. (In future chapters, we will be looking at each dimension in more depth.)
   a. Emotional dimension
   b. Volitional dimension (the will)
   c. Ethical dimension
   d. Intellectual dimension
   e. Spiritual dimension

2. Go around the group and share ideas of what it actually means to obey the top priority commandment and "Love the Lord, your God, with all your HEART." Refer to the dimensions of the HEART listed above.

3. Reflecting on the five dimensions of the HEART, share any new insights you have on what it means to respond to the familiar evangelical appeal, "give your HEART to Jesus."

4. Christ's call to effective discipleship is a call to develop a mature HEART and to work toward maturity in all five dimensions. Which dimension do you think is the area of greatest need for you personally at the moment? Describe the need.

5. Read 1 Corinthians 9:19–27. If you think of your spiritual journey as a race (as Paul did), describe the leg of the race you are now on. How do you think you should be training for it?

Session 5: The Volitional Dimension
(Chapter 4)

The first aspect of the HEART to be examined in detail is the volitional dimension—the will. I have chosen this place to begin because the confrontation of two wills—mine versus God's—brings into sharp focus the intensely personal nature of a relationship with Jesus Christ. As I follow my own progress, I can see the inevitable tension between opposing God's will and abandoning myself to it. But each time I surrender to what he wants for me, I sense a much greater reality—God's love for me personally and his love for the world of which I am a part. By acts of his will, God moves to express his love, and I find myself drawn to be a part of this expression in the high-tech world.

1. For personal reflection only: What difference would it make in your outlook on life if you *knew* what God had in mind when he created you and you were free to "go for it"?

2. Describe the first place you could call a "spiritual home." (Describe both the physical location and the people involved.)

3. When in your life did God first become more than just a word?

4. Where in your life has a "treasure" captured you and drawn you into a struggle to release that treasure to God?

5. When in your life have you come closest to "losing HEART" and giving up, refusing to go on?
6. Read Matthew 11:25–30 silently. As you read, consider the idea that Jesus is present in the room, speaking these words to you personally. In response to his invitation, what difficult tasks and heavy loads would you leave with him at this point in your life?
7. What would it mean for you personally to take up Christ's yoke and pick up his burden today?

Session 6: The Emotional Dimension
(Chapter 5)

The gospel accounts of the life of Jesus show him to be a person who had deep feelings and was not afraid to show them. (See, for example, John 11:35, the shortest verse in the Bible and dear to the hearts of small boys and trivia buffs: "Jesus wept.") Yet the high-tech world's motto seems to be: Don't talk! Don't think! Don't feel! It is clear from the New Testament record that a call to follow Christ is a call to emotional maturity.

1. We are sometimes aware and sometimes unaware of our own feelings. From the following list, pick one feeling of which you have been personally aware in the last week. Share it with the group.

love	resentment	happiness	reverence
hurt	excitement	humility	discouragement
discomfort	affection	amusement	cockiness
relief	fulfillment	confidence	need
anger	disgust	uneasiness	curiosity
shame	tension	joy	grief
anxiety	courage	hate	hopelessness
concern	sadness	guilt	awe
embarrassment	irritation	comfort	

2. Allow members of the group to point out one or more emotions they have observed in you over the past few weeks.
3. Read Matthew 6:25–27 silently. Share with the group one area of anxiety in your life at this moment. What do you think would happen if you could totally abandon this area to God?
4. Read Matthew 18:23–35. Share with the group an example from your life or the life of someone you know in which forgiveness of the

241

HEART could offer freedom from the compulsion to punish.

5. Read Matthew 12:28–34. On a practical level, what roadblocks does the world throw at you personally to prevent you from obeying these two top commandments in your everyday life?

Session 7: The Ethical Dimension
(Chapter 6)

The ethical dimension of the HEART is, for me, the most difficult to discuss. Ethics deal with good and evil in the world, and I find myself wanting to deny that evil exists. Life would be so much simpler that way. Even more important, I want to deny that the tension between good and evil exists *within my own life*. But the fact is that evil does exist in me, although Christ paid a great price on the cross to free me from its power. And it is my HEART that will determine the effect of both good and evil in my life.

In order to follow Christ as disciples in the high-tech world, we must become proficient at discerning good and evil. For example, some people believe technology is evil in and of itself. I do not agree. Technology itself is neither good nor evil, although it can be used to spread and multiply the effects of evil on the lives of people under its power. But technology can also be used to multiply and amplify the effects of good. The decision is made in the HEARTs of those who control the technology. And the same is true of countless other ethical issues we encounter in the high-tech world.

1. Have each group member share an example of evil that people have come to live with and accept as normal in the high-tech world around us.
2. Share with the group an example of technology that can be used either as a force for evil or a force for good.
3. Read Matthew 12:33–37. How can we use our own words and speech to monitor the presence of evil in our HEARTs? Share a recent example from your life or the life of someone you have observed.
4. Read Luke 8:5–15. Do you believe there is an Evil One who attempts to capture the HEART for evil? Explain why you believe as you do. Allow each group member to comment on the Evil One's strategy as described in this passage.
5. Read Matthew 5:8. What practical steps are open to us to purify our HEARTs of evil? Share a specific step you can take this coming week.

Session 8: The Intellectual Dimension
(Chapter 7)

The biblical concept of HEART includes the intellect. This fact puts to rest the idea of conflict between "the head" and "the heart," at least as far as the Bible is concerned.

In a very practical way, when Jesus Christ comes into our lives, we must abandon to him our intellects, as well as the other four dimensions of our HEARTs. At no time in history has it been more important than it is in the high-tech age to serve Christ with our intellects.

But what does it mean to abandon our intellects to Christ? Some Christians have acted as if it means you must check your brains at the door when you enter the church. But this chapter maintains that intellectual gifts, aptitudes, and abilities—however great or small—require faithful and disciplined development. The high-tech world awaits followers of Christ who understand both the world and God's ways and can use their minds to point Christ's way to others.

1. Allow each group member to share an example of antiintellectual biases and attitudes in the Christian community.
2. Again, poll each group member for examples of Christians who appear to be "intellectual snobs."
3. One definition of an "intellectual" is simply "one who knows." Share with the group an example where the sound thinking and knowledge of a particular Christian has helped you in your own Christian pilgrimage. (It may have come through talks, preaching, one-on-one conversations, or writing or other art forms.)
4. In what way do you sense God is calling you to develop your spiritual IQ and to gain a deeper understanding of God's will and ways, as well as opportunities for ministry in the high-tech world? What are some particular steps you can take in this direction?
5. Read Matthew 13:10–16. Is there some situation or area of your life in which you need to turn to God for insight and healing? (Be specific, but as brief or detailed as you like.)
6. Allow each person to construct a sentence prayer of petition around these seven verses. (You can write these out in your notebooks first, then share them in the group.)

Session 9: The Spiritual Dimension
(Chapter 8)

Several times in my life I have been involved in important and exciting scientific experiments and discoveries. But none of these have been more exciting to me than seeing Jesus Christ break into human life! In recent years, scientists have begun to talk publicly about the events in the universe that science may never be able to explain and that must be attributed to spiritual forces. Yet, for an individual human life the point of actual contact between God and man is the HEART.

It has always been possible to live with knowledge *about* God and not really *know* God. In the high-tech world, people are often exposed to spiritual values that are imbedded in our culture and yet never have experienced spiritual reality—the personal encounter with Jesus Christ in a life-changing experience. Regardless of how much attention is given to issues of the intellect, will, ethics, and emotions, I return to the question, "Is Christ real in my life now?" This is the challenge to *keep in touch* with God. There must be a daily discipline of the inward strategy if my HEART is to stay tuned in to God amid the roar and distractions of the high-tech age.

1. Go around the group and ask each person to share the areas of his life where it is easiest and most difficult to sense God's presence.
2. If you could begin your typical day with a one-sentence prayer that honestly expresses your true feelings to God, what would that sentence be?
3. If you could sit down for dinner with Jesus and receive an immediate answer to any pressing guidance question in your life, what would you ask him?
4. Read John 7:37–39. Allow a few moments to reflect on this passage and share one specific example of what it means for "living water" to flow out of your HEART in the week ahead.
5. Read Romans 12:1–8 aloud. Allow five minutes (have someone time it) for individual reflection on this passage and for listening for God's special word to each person out of the silence. Invite each member of the group to share his or her experience from the five minutes of listening.
6. Close the group by allowing each person to construct a one-sentence prayer of intercession based on Romans 12:1–8.

Session 10: An Exterior Strategy
(Chapter 9)

In this book, I have frequently used the phrase "follow Jesus Christ into the high-tech world." What does this mean for ordinary Christians who are not called to be religious professionals? The New Testament was vague about matters of ordination and other methods of setting people aside for special tasks. But it does give a clear picture—one we must recover today—of all Christ's followers busily engaged in work, service, and ministry as Christ's representatives. In part 3, we will examine some ideas of what it might mean to hear God's call to ministry in our families, congregations, daily work, and life in the community.

The challenge of following Jesus Christ into our world means that we must understand God's personal call to us and develop a strategy for doing what God asks us to do. And I believe that such a strategy means we must discover a new shape for lay ministry. Our job is not to assist the clergy in our churches; rather, the job of the clergy is to assist the laity in being about their ministry in the world. What shape will this ministry of ordinary lay men and women take?

1. If money were not an issue and you had all the time you needed, what would you like to do before you die?
2. Within your own world—your work, family, and community—what serious need or problem would you most like to see God break into this world and take care of?
3. Have you ever been tempted, drawn, or torn to leave the life you now live as an ordinary Christian for "full-time" Christian service? (If you *are* in "full-time" Christian service, reverse the question.) What was the result? How do you feel about your decision?
4. Share with the group one way your relationship with God has been strengthened (or could be strengthened) through the ordinary duties of your life.
5. Read Mark 5:1–20. How would you respond if Jesus spoke the command in verse 19 directly to you? Describe your message and your method in your own world of family, daily work, community, and congregation.

Session 11: Arena of the Church Scattered
(Chapter 10)

The central thought in part 3 is that the people of God are still the church from the time they leave the worship service on Sunday morning until they return to the sanctuary the following Sunday. This is what I call the Church Scattered. I believe the major challenge facing ordinary Christians today is the task of identifying and playing their roles in the Church Scattered out in the high-tech world Monday through Saturday.

When I search for my place as part of the Church Scattered, I must get in touch with my own spiritual gifts—the special gift or gifts placed in my life by the Holy Spirit. These gifts are valid and active all week long. We must also look at our vocations and ask, "What is God calling me to do?" We must face our call to our own families, our daily work, and our communities. We must ask what it means to *personally* follow Jesus Christ into the high-tech world.

1. In your imagination, picture your own workplace and family and select one person whose needs are real at this moment. If God could draw that person to you (because you are a Christian) and make it possible for you to select any gift for them, what would it be? (You can share the names with the group or not—whichever you prefer.)
2. In a practical sense, what is required of you actually to reach out to that person on Christ's behalf?
3. The leadership skills required to be Christ's person in the Church Scattered are in some ways simple and basic (as compared to the leadership skills required to direct the life of a congregation). What would it look and feel like to be a good, practical teacher or model of your faith—one who could show others how their faith actually works in the arena of daily work?
4. Select one practical thing you could do to demonstrate a "willingness to care for other people on Christ's behalf" in your daily work place and family?
5. Read 1 Timothy 3:1–7. If God gave you the gift of sharpening your leadership skills in the Church Scattered by eliminating a weakness and growing in a strength, what would you select? (The items may or may not be found in this passage.)
6. Think about the e-Leader as described in this chapter. According to this model, do you think *all* Christians are called to be this kind of leader? Why or why not?

Session 12: Arena of Daily Work
(Chapter 11)

Each person has a special place in life that is his or her place of daily work. This place could be tagged with many names—job, career, occupation, vocation, place of service. I have chosen to name this special place "daily work" because I believe it takes us to the most basic level of that arena of life, and because it includes people such as monks and homemakers who do not actually receive a paycheck for their efforts. I believe that our daily work is something to which God calls us each day—at least until he shows us something different and opens another door.

How do we serve Christ in our daily work in the high-tech age? This is a very serious question for all ordinary Christians in the Church Scattered. We must be accountable to God for both the kind of work we do and the way we do our work. In addition, it is important for Christ in some way to become real in our work arena and begin to draw people to himself through us. Is there one style of doing things that is most effective in the work arena? I believe there is—the style of a servant which Jesus modeled for us.

1. How would you describe your daily work to someone who knew nothing about it? (What? Where? When? How? Why?)
2. Reread Merton's comment on work on page 156. How would you characterize your own work style? In what area of your daily work can God most easily get your attention?
3. Use your imagination to construct the profile and role of a servant leader in your personal work arena. What would it feel like to be in this role?
4. Read Colossians 3:23. Describe how you would apply this verse to your own daily work. Do you *feel* that it is important to God for you to do this?
5. Do you feel that you are investing your God-given talents and abilities in the most effective way possible? What options could make your stewardship of your life more effective?
6. Read Ezekiel 31:10–11 and 33:30–33. How would you describe God's formula for success in your daily work? How do you personally feel about leaving the amount and kinds of rewards for your daily work in God's hands?

Session 13: Arena of Government
(Chapter 12)

Perhaps some of my readers have lived under forms of government which differ markedly from mine in the United States. I have lived my entire life with a system of city, county, state, and federal governments that requires and allows my participation as a citizen of a democracy. I have never had my right to practice the Christian faith blocked by a government. So sometimes I must be reminded that I take for granted rights and freedoms that are not available to Christians everywhere. Even within my own country, there are people who have more difficulty claiming these rights and freedoms than I have had.

Following Christ in the arena of government means that I must discover what it means to be a citizen as the high-tech age allows the government to play greater and greater roles in the lives of all the people. To do this effectively, I must understand the biblical concept of governments which establish order so that God can work creatively in the arenas of family, work, and church.

1. Describe the governments (local through federal) under which you have lived in your lifetime. Give an example of the most effective and the least effective.
2. Give one example where your government's inability to establish and maintain order has posed a threat or a problem for you or your family.
3. Read Acts 16:25–40. How can a government allow free passage for the gospel of Jesus Christ and still not forcibly impose religion on the people it governs?
4. Give one example of a problem area involving families in your country and describe how the government helps or fails to help. What could be done to allow God to work creatively in this situation?
5. Give one example of a problem area involving the work arena in your country and describe how the government helps or fails to help. What could be done to allow God to work creatively to resolve the crisis?
6. Read Acts 26:24–32 and 1 Kings 3:5–9. In what way can a "hearing HEART" guide you personally to witness and action in the community where you live? To what areas of concern do you think he is calling you?

Session 14: Arena of the Church Gathered
(Chapter 13)

In the high-tech age, ordinary Christians will most likely continue to be gathered together in congregations. But what style must a congregation develop to equip and support lay ministry in the high-tech age? I believe that lay men and women will take an increasingly active role in defining congregational priorities and devising an agenda designed to meet the needs of lay ministers in the congregation.

As I consider my own role in my church for the coming year, I begin to wonder how I can best serve Christ in the Church Gathered. This is a question for all of us. What can make the difference between exciting, effective ministry and humdrum (even boring) busy work at the church? We must seek ways to work the principles of this chapter into our own lives. We must seek ways to fan the flames of lay ministry in the world from the live coals of renewed congregations alive in Jesus Christ.

1. What evidence do you have of your congregation's commitment to the ministry of ordinary Christians, the laity? How would you rate your congregation's efforts in this area?
2. What tensions and frustrations have you personally encountered in trying to put your gifts to work through service and ministry in the

congregation? How could the congregational leaders help you become more effective?

3. Name one area where you feel your congregation has achieved excellence in its ministry and one area that needs to be confronted and shaped up.

4. Is your congregation clear about what its ministry should be? Suggest one idea that would sharpen the congregation's strategy for ministry in the high-tech age.

5. Describe your personal creative dream of what your congregation would be like if tonight a fresh new convenant was struck for God to be Lord of the church and all the people convenanted to a new level of obedience and service under Christ. What programs would be kept, revised, or discarded? What new ideas would you put to work? (Remember the estimate that, if the Holy Spirit were removed from the church, 90 percent of the activities would continue and we would be proud of them!)

6. Close with each person praying a prayer of intercession for his or her own congregation after reflecting on Jeremiah 24:6–7.

Session 15: Arena of the Family
(Chapter 14)

Few tasks are as scary and challenging in the high-tech age as building and maintaining a family. And very few ventures today have as high a risk of failure. All too often, the families of the high-tech age have been abandoned to the devastating effects of pornography, recreational sex, drugs, and alcohol. Parents today often give their children every conceivable gift except the one they are searching for—a valid purpose for being alive.

The biblical concept of family is a small community where parents are chartered by God to lead their children to a meaningful life through a personal relationship with Jesus Christ. But how can this task be approached when it runs counter to the prevailing culture of the high-tech age? Where can we find direction and guidance for this kind of family life? I believe the family must become a microscopic model of the body of Christ—the smallest element of Christian community where people are loved and accepted as sinners saved by grace. The family must revolve around God's love and acceptance.

1. Describe the house where you lived as a child and the family you grew up in.

2. Describe the center of warmth in that house and in the family. What person or activity made you feel happy and loved? If your home

life was unhappy and you have trouble with this question, describe a kind of family life you always wanted or dreamed about.

3. Describe the family you are a part of today and the person you feel you are closest to in your family unit. (This doesn't have to be the traditional "nuclear family" if that term doesn't apply to you. It could be an extended family or even an adopted family.)

4. In what ways does your current family approach the family model of a small Christian community based on love and unearned acceptance? In what ways is it different? (This may not be an easy question, since many families in the high-tech age are under severe stress.)

5. It has been said that Christ is not only a mediator between God and persons but also between people. Suggest ways in which this mediation can make practical differences between a husband and wife or members of a family. Share a practical personal example of how this principle works (or should work) for you.

6. Read Mark 7:18–23. What practical defenses are available to defend a marriage and a family against their natural enemies described by Jesus in this passage?

Session 16: Clusters
(Chapter 15)

The distinguishing mark of a "cluster" is a commitment to growth of the HEART and growth in effective ministry and service in the high-tech world. Each person's starting point may be different. Each person's call may be unique. But it is Christ who calls ordinary Christians, and a "cluster" group can be the base camp and support center for launching such ordinary Christians out to be Christ's people wherever he has placed them. The only place Christ can't use us is where we aren't!

My hope, of course, is that each group of people who study this book together can become a cluster—a special place for growing HEARTs and increasing effectiveness in ministry. But I have found that a cluster must have three key ingredients if growth is to occur: vulnerability, confrontation, and affirmation. The following questions are intended to allow you to sample the style of the "catacombs" cluster described in chapter 15 and to perform a self-evaluation of the three key growth-producing ingredients.

1. Go around the group and let each person describe the single most important personal problem, crisis, issue, and/or challenge of the past week—and the one anticipated for the coming week.

2. Go around the group a second time and give each person an opportunity to share what difference having Christ a part of these experiences makes.
3. Allow each person to share his or her own opinion of the importance of affirmation in a group like yours. Has there been a point where affirmation helped or could have helped your group?
4. Go around again and let each person give his or her opinion on the importance of vulnerability in a group like yours. Has there been a point where vulnerability helped or could have helped the group?
5. Repeat this process for confrontation, and again cite an example where confrontation helped or could have helped.
6. Read Luke 5:1–11. Search the story of this first encounter between Jesus and Peter for examples of vulnerability, confrontation, and affirmation that led Peter into a new kind of personal growth as a disciple.

Session 17: The Focus
(Epilogue)

The prologue pointed to a mountain-climbing experience as a model for the challenge faced by ordinary Christians who commit to follow Jesus Christ in the age of high technology. We have explored the high-tech age, the inward strategy of the HEART, and the external strategy for discipleship in today's world. But there are so many things to do and so little time to get things done! God's lesson for me as I shared my friend's death from cancer is that the time is short, so we need to get our priorities straight and focus on the key issues.

As the church contemplates its role in the high-tech world, the time *is* short. As we, the laity, ponder our role in the church, the time *is* short. The high-tech world propels us forward at higher and higher speeds. Yet, with all our understanding of the HEART and the world, we must still face the challenge of discovering the shape of our own obedience to Jesus Christ—one day at a time. We must each stand, once again, facing the mountain—this time with our climbing team—and ask, "Lord, what is the next step you would have me take?"

1. Share with the group the next step you feel God is asking you to take in your interior strategy to develop your HEART. (Allow five minutes of silence before you begin sharing.)
2. Share with the group the next step you feel God is calling you to take in following Christ in your congregation.
3. Finally, share the next step God is asking you to take as you set out to follow Christ in the high-tech world.

4. Read John 1:1–4. If the focus of the entire Christian enterprise is a *common shared life* with Jesus Christ and those who know and serve him, what practical steps can you take to link your life with partners who will "rope together" with you as you respond to God's call to you?

5. What must you personally abandon to God in order to step out with Christ to discover the unique shape of your ministry and service as Christ's person in the high-tech world?

About The Author:

DR. ROBERT SLOCUM is both an "ordinary Christian"—a Presbyterian layman—and a high-tech entrepreneur—the founder and president of Polatomic, Inc., a Dallas, Texas, company which specializes in consulting on high-technology new product development and manufacture of laser optical components. An atomic physicist, he has worked in such high-tech fields as oil exploration, space exploration, and laser systems. He has also been active in the church over the last 25 years as a teacher, lay witness, and retreat leader. He has served as Coordinator of Lay Renewal Conferences in Presbyterian churches across the South and in 1984 he was Program Co-Chairman for the National Presbyterian Congress on Renewal. He currently serves as ruling elder in the Highland Park Presbyterian Church in Dallas. Dr. Slocum and his wife, Linda, live in Richardson, Texas, with their son, Paul.